BLITZ CATALOGING WORKBOOK
SUBJECT ANALYSIS

Other Blitz Cataloging Workbooks

MARC/AACR2/Authority Control Tagging
Cataloging Nonprint Materials

BLITZ CATALOGING WORKBOOK

SUBJECT ANALYSIS

Bobby Ferguson

1998
Libraries Unlimited, Inc.
Englewood, Colorado

Copyright © 1998 Libraries Unlimited, Inc.
All Rights Reserved
Printed in the United States of America

No part of this publication may be reproduced, stored in a retrieval system, or transmitted, in any form or by any means, electronic, mechanical, photocopying, recording, or otherwise, without the prior written permission of the publisher.

LIBRARIES UNLIMITED, INC.
P.O. Box 6633
Englewood, CO 80155-6633
(800) 237-6124
www.lu.com

Constance Hardesty, *Project Manager*
Brooke Graves, *Editor*
Sheryl Tongue, *Design and Composition*

Suggested cataloging:

Ferguson, Bobby.
    Subject analysis : blitz cataloging workbook / Bobby Ferguson.
    xi, 135 p. 22×28 cm.
    Includes bibliographical references (p. 95) and index.
    ISBN 1-56308-645-X
    1. Subject cataloging--United States--Rules--Problems, exercises, etc.
  I. Title. II. Blitz cataloging workbook.
Z695 1998
025.47--dc21

P

> In order to keep this title in print and available to the academic community, this edition was produced using digital reprint technology in a relatively short print run. This would not have been attainable using traditional methods. Although the cover has been changed from its original appearance, the text remains the same and all materials and methods used still conform to the highest book-making standards.

Table of Contents

Acknowledgments, vii

Overview of the Blitz Cataloging Workbooks, ix

Introduction, xi

1. *Library of Congress Subject Headings*, 1
    1.1   *LCSH* Subject Heading Exercises, 2
    1.2   *LCSH* Subject Heading Terminology Exercises, 8
    1.3   *LCSH* Geographic Subdivisions Exercises, 11
    1.4   Pattern Headings, 14
    1.5   Inverted Heading versus Subdivision or Phrase Heading Exercises, 18
    1.6   Annotated Card Program Exercises, 19
    1.7   Scope Notes, 21
          LCSH Scope Note Exercises, 21
    1.8   *Subject Cataloging Manual: Subject Headings* and *Free-Floating Subdivisions: An Alphabetical Index*, 22
          Subject Cataloging Manual and *Free-Floating Subdivisions* Exercises, 23
    1.9   Subdivisions on History, 26
          LCSH History Subdivisions Exercises, 27
    1.10 Biography Subdivisions, 30
    1.11 Bible Headings and Subdivisions, 35
    1.12 Special Subdivisions from *SCM:SH*, 38

2. *Sears List of Subject Headings*, 43
    2.1   *Sears* Subject Heading Exercises, 43
    2.2   *Sears* Subject Heading Terminology and Scope Notes, 50
    2.3   *Sears* History Subdivisions, 54
          Sears History Subdivisions Exercises, 54

3. *Dewey Decimal Classification*, 59
   Introduction, 59
    3.1   Dewey Relative Index Exercises, 59
    3.2   Dewey Schedules Exercises, 62
    3.3   Number Building from Schedules, 66
          Number Building Exercises, 67
    3.4   Number Building from Tables, 71
          Number Building from Tables Exercises, 72

3.5 Cutter Numbers, 79
Cutter Table Exercises, 79

4. Library of Congress Classification, 83
Introduction, 83
Library of Congress Classifications, 85
Cutter Table, 86
4.1 LCC Author Cutter Exercises, 87
4.2 LCC Outline Exercises, 88
4.3 LCC Exercises, Set 1, 89
4.4 LCC Exercises, Set 2, 92

Bibliography, 95

Answer Key, 97

Acknowledgments

I would like to express my appreciation and gratitude to Tom Jaques, Mickey McKann, and Elisabeth Spanhoff of the State Library of Louisiana; Anna Marchiafava of the West Baton Rouge Parish Library; Michael Carpenter of the LSU School of Library and Information Science; Dominique Hallet, Terre Ferguson, and Anna Wade for inspiration; Sandy Colby and Dave and Carol Wines for graphics and computer help; Gary Ferguson for help with the wording and proofing, and for his continuing friendship; and my editor, Sheila Intner, for all her help, friendship, and knowledge. Thank you all.

BLITZ CATALOGING WORKBOOKS
Overview

Cataloging and classification are the most important parts of librarianship. Without a catalog, either manual or electronic, a library is no more than a room full of books and cannot provide services to its patrons in a reliable, timely fashion. Other library activities such as acquisition of new materials, interlibrary lending, and reference cannot be accomplished if patrons and staff cannot find out what a particular library contains.

Knowledge of cataloging is important to all librarians, not just catalogers. As more and more libraries become automated, a knowledge of MARC fields and electronic formats, as well as call numbers and subject headings, is essential and will make all librarians more proficient. Using these workbooks should cause you to absorb a lot of information that will be useful to you in any library situation.

As for catalogers, you will find that you cannot do a superior job as a beginning cataloger. Experience is necessary, preferably under an experienced cataloger. These workbooks are intended to reinforce your knowledge of the fundamentals of cataloging. They will help you to understand the MARC format and functions of the various fields and subfields; to evaluate copy cataloging and classification of various formats of materials; to locate errors and inconsistencies; to learn access points and which are the most important; to assign subject headings using both *Library of Congress Subject Headings* and *Sears List of Subject Headings*; to assign call numbers in both Dewey and LC classification schedules; and to evaluate and construct cross-references and authority headings.

SUBJECT ANALYSIS
Introduction

Subject analysis in a bibliographic record consists of two elements—a call number and subject headings. These two components are completely different, but must agree with each other to identify the subject matter of a given item properly and to give best access to the information contained with it. A book or other work with a call number for cookery and subject headings for history of Outer Mongolia would be totally confusing to users, and cause the real subject of the book to be obscured. An incorrect classification number, irrelevant subject headings, or missing subject headings may cause the book to be lost forever, and the money spent on acquiring, cataloging, and shelving it will be completely wasted. In addition, good subject analysis will assist reference librarians as well as patrons to make the best possible use of the collection.

There are two primary schemes of classification used in the United States and in Canada (Dewey Decimal classification system and Library of Congress classification), and two primary sets of subject heading material (*Sears List of Subject Headings* and *Library of Congress Subject Headings*). This workbook will cover all four of these tools in order to accommodate the needs of small school, public, and special librarians as well as those in large public or academic libraries.

Subject heading exercises are compiled using the 20th edition of *Library of Congress Subject Headings* and the 16th edition of *Sears List of Subject Headings*.

Classification exercises are compiled using DDC21 (©1996) and the latest volumes for each subject of the LCC scheme.

1.
LIBRARY OF CONGRESS SUBJECT HEADINGS

The Library of Congress has a very large collection of materials—books, manuscripts, and nonprint materials of all kinds. An essential tool for providing systematic access to this collection is the *Library of Congress Subject Headings (LCSH)*, first issued in 1909. The 20th edition is available in a four-volume set totaling over 6,000 pages, on microfiche, CD-ROM, and online.

The Library of Congress issues updates between editions in the *Library of Congress Subject Headings Weekly Lists* and in the *Cataloging Service Bulletin* (or *CSB*), a quarterly publication put out by the Cataloging Policy and Support Office to disseminate information relating to cataloging matters. The *Weekly Lists* contain the full records with all cross-references, whereas the *CSB* contains only the main headings. It also contains lists of the new headings approved for use during the quarter, changed or deleted headings, and topical headings that have been changed to name headings.

The *Library of Congress Subject Headings* is a very versatile tool. However, catalogers are not allowed to alter these headings or to create new ones, though sometimes they may wish to do so. For example, some headings are subdivided geographically (most topical headings) and some are not (place headings such as **Mule Canyon Wilderness (Utah)** or fictitious characters such as **Mulcahy, Kate (Fictitious character)**). Family names also cannot be subdivided by place, but you *are* allowed to subdivide the place by --**Biography** or --**Genealogy**. So, although **Bourgeois family** cannot be subdivided by --**Louisiana**, you can use both **Bourgeois family** *and* **Louisiana--Genealogy** in order to identify properly the subject of the work.

Some headings are created as patterns; for example, the pattern heading for diseases is **Cancer** and all diseases may be subdivided by the same subtopics as are used under **Cancer**. If all main headings were to duplicate the subdivisions listed under the pattern headings, *LCSH* would be even larger and more expensive to produce and purchase.

Under an established heading, cross-references to other headings—narrower terms, broader terms, and related terms—are also provided. By browsing the relevant headings you may find others more appropriate for the item being cataloged.

Another useful item given with many *LCSH* main headings is a suggested LC classification number. For those libraries using the LC classification scheme, this is a helpful shortcut.

Children's materials, and indeed children's collections, need shorter, and easier-to-use, subject headings than do adult materials. The Annotated Card Program was designed to be used with children's materials, although any heading in *LCSH* may be used. When adult headings are used, a subdivision such as --**Juvenile literature** or --**Juvenile fiction** may have to be added.

2 *Library of Congress Subject Headings*

The Library of Congress created the *Subject Cataloging Manual: Subject Headings* to assist Library of Congress catalogers. So many libraries began using it that it has been altered to meet the needs of more than just the Library of Congress. *Free-Floating Subdivisions: An Alphabetical Index*, now in annual editions, accompanies the *Manual* and is also very useful as a cataloging tool. Using the *Subject Cataloging Manual: Subject Headings* and the *Free-Floating Subdivisions* will make a cataloger's work easier and more precise.

The size and complexity of *LCSH* can seem overwhelming at first glance. The following exercises are designed to help you learn to use it easily and competently.

In the pages that follow are exercises testing your knowledge of these tools and their application to library materials. They are designed to supplement training or coursework that teaches these principles and practices. The workbook is not intended to be a textbook, and sometimes gives instructions to use other works in addition to the information given here in order to complete the exercises.

1.1. *LCSH* Subject Heading Exercises

List three subject headings from *Library of Congress Subject Headings* which you could assign for books on the topics listed below. In a work situation you may assign more or less than three, but for this exercise come up with three for each topic. You will need to use free-floating subdivisions; see the *Subject Cataloging Manual: Subject Headings* and its *Index*.

1.1.1. A biography of Huey Long.

   A. _____

   B. _____

   C. _____

1.1.2. A history of the Louisiana State Department of Education from 1850 to 1950.

   A. _____

   B. _____

   C. _____

1.1.3. Tunica-Biloxi Indian tribal customs.

   A. _____

   B. _____

   C. _____

1.1.4. Black soldiers who took part in the Civil War.

   A. _____

   B. _____

   C. _____

1.1.5. Plantations and plantation life in New Orleans.

   A. _____

   B. _____

   C. _____

1.1.6. Oil leases in the Gulf of Mexico.

   A. _____

   B. _____

   C. _____

1.1.7. Prize-winning library buildings in Louisiana.

   A. _____

   B. _____

   C. _____

1.1.8. A genealogy of the Hebert family of New Orleans.

   A. _____

   B. _____

   C. _____

1.1.9. Legal status of hazardous waste disposal in salt domes.

   A. _____

   B. _____

   C. _____

4 Library of Congress Subject Headings

1.1.10. Public hearing for a road project in Cobb County, Georgia.

　　A. _____

　　B. _____

　　C. _____

1.1.11. Flood damage reduction project in Johnstown, Pennsylvania.

　　A. _____

　　B. _____

　　C. _____

1.1.12. Schools and school attendance in Louisiana's Florida Parishes in the 18th century.

　　A. _____

　　B. _____

　　C. _____

1.1.13. History of Arpadhon, a Hungarian settlement in southeast Louisiana.

　　A. _____

　　B. _____

　　C. _____

1.1.14. Political situation in Sarajevo.

　　A. _____

　　B. _____

　　C. _____

1.1.15. Troop movements in Operation Desert Storm.

　　A. _____

　　B. _____

　　C. _____

1.1. LCSH Subject Heading Exercises 5

1.1.16. Printing presses in 18th-century Germany.

    A. _____

    B. _____

    C. _____

1.1.17. Case studies of persons with AIDS.

    A. _____

    B. _____

    C. _____

1.1.18. Debate on euthanasia.

    A. _____

    B. _____

    C. _____

1.1.19. A history of the Great Wall of China.

    A. _____

    B. _____

    C. _____

1.1.20. A biography of Richard Nixon.

    A. _____

    B. _____

    C. _____

1.1.21. Plantation life in the area around Richmond, Virginia.

    A. _____

    B. _____

    C. _____

1.1.22. A history of the Missoula, Montana, Mayor's Office.

   A. _____

   B. _____

   C. _____

1.1.23. Cherokee Indian marriage customs.

   A. _____

   B. _____

   C. _____

1.1.24. List of veterans from Alabama who fought in the Civil War.

   A. _____

   B. _____

   C. _____

1.1.25. Alaskan pipelines and their construction and maintenance.

   A. _____

   B. _____

   C. _____

1.1.26. Encyclopedia of Louisiana irises.

   A. _____

   B. _____

   C. _____

1.1.27. Legal issues in junk bond trading.

   A. _____

   B. _____

   C. _____

1.1. *LCSH* Subject Heading Exercises   7

1.1.28. A genealogy of the Whitefield family of Shawnee, Kansas.

   A. _____
   B. _____
   C. _____

1.1.29. Damage by Hurricane Andrew in Florida and Louisiana.

   A. _____
   B. _____
   C. _____

1.1.30. Freight traffic on the Erie Canal during the 19th century.

   A. _____
   B. _____
   C. _____

1.1.31. Relationships between the Isletos and the settlers in New Mexico.

   A. _____
   B. _____
   C. _____

1.1.32. Public hearing for a proposed new Mississippi River bridge at St. Louis, Missouri.

   A. _____
   B. _____
   C. _____

1.1.33. Repair of all-terrain vehicles, particularly dune buggies and snowmobiles.

   A. _____
   B. _____
   C. _____

8 *Library of Congress Subject Headings*

1.1.34. Mount Everest climbing expeditions.

A. _____

B. _____

C. _____

1.1.35. A biography of Anthony Panizzi.

A. _____

B. _____

C. _____

1.1.36. Design and construction of cupolas and other decorative roof details.

A. _____

B. _____

C. _____

1.2. *LCSH* Subject Heading Terminology Exercises

1.2.1. List the narrower terms given under the heading **Antibiotics in agriculture.**

1.2.2. List the broader terms given under the heading **Genioplasty.**

1.2.3. List the terms that may be used in addition to the given term under the heading **Mediterranean race.**

1.2.4. List the terms that you may NOT use under the heading **Tansy ragwort.**

1.2.5. List the subdivisions that you may use under the heading **Machine shops.**

1.2. LCSH Subject Heading Terminology Exercises

1.2.6. List the subdivisions that you may NOT use under the heading **Insurance, Health**.

1.2.7. May the heading **American ginseng** be subdivided geographically?

1.2.8. May the heading **Fuglestad family** be subdivided geographically?

1.2.9. May the heading **Fuerte River (Mexico)** be subdivided geographically?

1.2.10. List other headings that might be used in place of **Berg family**.

1.2.11. List other headings that might also be used with **Berries**.

1.2.12. Are there any other headings listed for use under **Bessarabia (Moldova and Ukraine)**?

1.2.13. Are there any subdivisions listed for use under **Gesture**?

1.2.14. How many narrower terms are listed under the heading **Art**?

1.2.15. Give the common name of **Spine**, which is not used as a subject heading.

1.2.16. List a broader term and a narrower term for the heading **Tar**.

1.2.17. Are there any terms you cannot use for a treatise on expurgated books?

1.2.18. Does **Black nationalism** have a related term?

1.2.19. What are the broader terms suggested under **Industrial toxicology**?

1.2.20. Which one of the terms from question #1.2.19 would be more appropriate for **Black Lung Disease**?

1.2.21. Does **Orders of knighthood and chivalry--Insignia** have broader or narrower terms?

1.2.22. Do either of the two terms from question #1.2.21 have a scope note giving a definition?

1.2.23. Does the broader term given under the heading **Franklin Court (Philadelphia, Pa.)** help you understand what the heading means? How?

1.2.24. What is a narrower term for *Spizaetus*?

1.2.25. Give the broader terms for **Burchell's zebra**.

1.3. *LCSH* Geographic Subdivisions Exercises

The exercises here give topics that need both subject headings and geographic subdivisions. Some will also need topical subdivisions as well. Write your answers in the space provided, giving full *LCSH* subject headings from the 20th edition.

1.3.1. Current laws concerning industrial design in Kansas City, Kansas.

1.3.2. Native folk art drawings of a Tibetan monk who resides in Paris.

1.3.3. Occupational guidance for carpentry as taught in Milwaukee.

1.3.4. Laws governing protection of wildlife in Georgia.

1.3.5. A history of the Gamgee family from Norman, Oklahoma.

1.3.6. History and criticism of film editing in Bombay.

1.3.7. Humorous anecdotes about schools in the 19th century in Utah.

1.3.8. Design of crawfish molds for Louisiana cooking.

1.3.9. A plan for defense measures in industries in Nebraska.

1.3.10. A genealogical account of the Shanholtz family of New Jersey.

1.3.11. A catalog of videocassettes on anthropology in China.

1.3.12. Piano recitals in Hamburg, Germany.

1.3.13. Deer hunting in Colorado.

1.3.14. Presidential election results from the Republic of South Africa.

1.3.15. Log rolling contests in the Yukon.

1.3.16. The building of the Alaska Pipeline.

1.3.17. Low-fat refried bean recipes from Laredo.

1.3.18. Breeding farms in Kentucky for Belgian draft horses.

1.3.19. Transportation of explosives through Kansas City, Missouri.

1.3.20. Behavior modification of problem adolescents in New York City.

1.3.21. Right-to-life movement in New Brunswick, New Jersey.

1.3.22. Treatment of animals in Omaha, Nebraska.

1.3.23. Nesting habits of the great spotted woodpecker in Boise.

1.3.24. Directory of French naval stations in Europe.

1.3.25. French forgeries of Vienna porcelain.

1.3.26. Directory of studios dealing with color separation in Oahu, Hawaii.

1.3.27. Textbook on fossil invertebrates of ancient China.

1.3.28. Photographic identification of phlebobranchia in Chile.

1.3.29. Manual on growing quick-cooking rice in Louisiana.

1.3.30. History of the Los Angeles cult that venerates angels.

1.3.31. Textbook on Jukun grammar of Nigeria.

1.3.32. Policy manual for Japanese littleneck clam fishery on Cape Cod.

1.3.33. Umbrella industry in Seattle, Washington.

1.4. Pattern Headings

Pattern headings are established to conserve space. Certain standardized sets of topical and form subdivisions are developed for use under particular categories of subject headings. These subdivisions are then printed in full under one or two representative headings from each category, and are appropriate for use with other headings in the same category. For example, the category **Musical instruments** has a full set of subdivisions under the topic **Piano**, which is the *pattern heading* for musical instruments. --**Practicing** is not listed under **Clarinet**, but is nevertheless a valid subdivision for use with **Clarinet** because it is listed under **Piano**, the pattern heading for musical instruments. Read the section on pattern headings in the introduction to the *Library of Congress Subject Headings* on p. xiii of the 20th edition.

1.4.1. A discussion of the history of Cajun French as a language.

Basic subject _____

Pattern heading to be used _____

Full subject heading _____

1.4.2. Road testing of frost-resistant concrete in south Louisiana.

Basic subject _____

Pattern heading to be used _____

Full subject heading _____

1.4.3. A book on how to get your lambs pedigreed.

Basic subject _____

Pattern heading to be used _____

Full subject heading _____

1.4.4. Disclosure of corruption in the oil and gas industry in Texas.

Basic subject _____

Pattern heading to be used _____

Full subject heading _____

1.4. Pattern Headings   15

1.4.5. Research on the genetic aspects of myasthenia gravis.

Basic subject _____

Pattern heading to be used _____

Full subject heading _____

1.4.6. A guide to Lord Byron's home in Venice. *[Hint: name heading is Byron, George Gordon Byron, Baron.]*

Basic subject _____

Pattern heading to be used _____

Full subject heading _____

1.4.7. A book of photographs showing the migration of wildebeests in Africa.

Basic subject _____

Pattern heading to be used _____

Full subject heading _____

1.4.8. A book on the health of the Baptist preachers of Los Angeles.

Basic subject _____

Pattern heading to be used _____

Full subject heading _____

1.4.9. A handbook on harbor defenses in Hong Kong.

Basic subject _____

Pattern heading to be used _____

Full subject heading _____

1.4.10. A price guide to antique harps.

Basic subject _____

Pattern heading to be used _____

Full subject heading _____

16 *Library of Congress Subject Headings*

1.4.11. A conference on pests attacking wheat fields in Rapides Parish, Louisiana.

Basic subject _____

Pattern heading to be used _____

Full subject heading _____

1.4.12. Boundary disputes in the French colonies in America.

Basic subject _____

Pattern heading to be used _____

Full subject heading _____

1.4.13. Customs and practices of the Franciscans.

Basic subject _____

Pattern heading to be used _____

Full subject heading _____

1.4.14. Personnel in ground support of the Royal Canadian Air Force.

Basic subject _____

Pattern heading to be used _____

Full subject heading _____

1.4.15. Cavalry operations in the Spanish-American War.

Basic subject _____

Pattern heading to be used _____

Full subject heading _____

1.4.16. Compliance costs in medical malpractice suits.

Basic subject _____

Pattern heading to be used _____

Full subject heading _____

1.4. Pattern Headings   17

1.4.17. Oxidation tendencies in quartz in Seattle.

   Basic subject _____

   Pattern heading to be used _____

   Full subject heading _____

1.4.18. Psychosomatic aspects of colon diseases.

   Basic subject _____

   Pattern heading to be used _____

   Full subject heading _____

1.4.19. Capitalization practices in the Monghol language.

   Basic subject _____

   Pattern heading to be used _____

   Full subject heading _____

1.4.20. American influences on Tibetan literature.

   Basic subject _____

   Pattern heading to be used _____

   Full subject heading _____

1.4.21. Use of punctuation in the works of Eudora Welty.

   Basic subject _____

   Pattern heading to be used _____

   Full subject heading _____

1.4.22. Measurement of the moisture content in asphalt pavements.

   Basic subject _____

   Pattern heading to be used _____

   Full subject heading _____

1.4.23. Body alignment in humvees.

Basic subject _____

Pattern heading to be used _____

Full subject heading _____

1.5. Inverted Heading versus Subdivision or Phrase Heading Exercises

The Library of Congress is making an effort to change inverted headings (**Shops, Job**) to phrase headings (**Job shops**) or a heading --subheading (**Presidents, American** to **Presidents -- United States**) where appropriate. You must consult *LCSH* to see which way the heading is correctly written. Put a check beside the correct subject heading.

1.5.1. _____ Newspapers, American.
_____ Newspapers--United States.

1.5.2. _____ Folklore, Ukrainian.
_____ Folklore--Ukraine.

1.5.3. _____ Ballads, English.
_____ English ballads.

1.5.4. _____ French literature.
_____ Literature, French.

1.5.5. _____ Presidents, French.
_____ Presidents--France.

1.5.6. _____ Newspapers, German.
_____ German newspapers.

1.5.7. _____ Periodicals, Mongolian.
_____ Mongolian periodicals.

1.5.8. _____ Players, Bridge.
_____ Bridge players.

1.5.9. _____ Cookery, German.
_____ German cookery.

1.5.10. _____ Thinking, Divergent.
_____ Divergent thinking.

1.5.11. _____ Mediation, Divorce.
_____ Divorce mediation.

1.5.12. ____ Families, Black.
____ Black families.

1.5.13. ____ Hazard, Frost.
____ Frost hazard.

1.5.14. ____ Poetry--Guatemala.
____ Guatemalan poetry.

1.5.15. ____ Haggadot, Kibbutz.
____ Kibbutz Haggadot.

1.5.16. ____ Iron sculpture, Buddhist.
____ Buddhist iron sculpture.

1.5.17. ____ John, the Baptist, Saint.
____ Saint John the Baptist.

1.5.18. ____ Navies, Cost of.
____ Cost of navies.

1.5.19. ____ Coatings, Protective.
____ Protective coatings.

1.5.20. ____ Proteins--Denaturation.
____ Protein denaturation.

1.5.21. ____ Railroads--Train dispatching.
____ Train dispatching.

1.5.22. ____ Rosettes, Barite.
____ Barite rosettes.

1.5.23. ____ Respiration, Artificial.
____ Artificial respiration.

1.5.24. ____ Restorations, Political.
____ Political restorations.

1.6. Annotated Card Program Exercises

Read the section on pages AC-i to AC-iv in volume 1 of *LCSH*, 20th ed. Use the list of headings on pages AC-1 to AC-15 to answer the following questions.

1.6.1. List the narrower terms given under the heading **Amusements**.

20 Library of Congress Subject Headings

1.6.2. List the broader terms given under the heading **Birds as pets**.

1.6.3. List the terms that may be used instead of **Birth**.

1.6.4. List the terms that you may NOT use under the heading **Bridge (Game)**.

1.6.5. List the subdivisions that you may use under the heading **English language**.

1.6.6. List the subdivisions that you may NOT use under the heading **English language**.

1.6.7. Can the heading **Folklore** be subdivided geographically?

1.6.8. List other headings that might be used in place of **Magic tricks**.

1.6.9. Which heading could you use for a story book told in rhyming format?

1.6.10. Which heading could you use for a book where you choose the plot?

1.6.11. Would you include the subdivision --**Juvenile literature** after any of the headings referred to in questions #1.6.9 and #1.6.10?

1.6.12. What is the difference between the heading used for a mystery story in the Annotated Card Program and the adult list?

1.6.13. What subject heading would you use for folklore of the Altai peoples?

1.6.14. What subject heading would you use for the creation of animated films?

1.6.15. If you wanted to use the subject heading **Church history** for a juvenile book, what would you have to do?

1.6.16. What subject heading would you use for juvenile short stories about boxing in the Annotated Card Program? For adult short stories about boxing?

1.6.17. Does the scope note under **Cartoons and comics** limit you, or give you additional entries to make?

1.7. Scope Notes

Scope notes are given to enhance the cataloger's understanding of the subject heading being considered. Sometimes the scope note limits the use of the heading, as in **Economic forecasting**, or defines the geographical area, as in **Southwest, New**. A new or unfamiliar term is sometimes broadly defined (for example, **Artists' preparatory studies**). Some terms will have reciprocal scope notes; see **Life on other planets** and **Extraterrestial anthropology** for an example of this type of note. Some headings require a second subject heading in addition to the one chosen. **School prose**, for example, if subdivided geographically and pertaining to a single school, must also have the name of the school as a subject heading.

Scope notes were placed in *LCSH* to assist the cataloger, and should be read whenever they are found. They will give the cataloger options that otherwise may be missed.

LCSH Scope Note Exercises

Write the answer to each question in the space provided.

1.7.1. How should the heading **Fishing guides** be used?

1.7.2. Is there a reciprocal scope note under **Husband and wife**?

1.7.3. Is there a scope note under **Blues (Music)**?

1.7.4. What type of scope note is given under **Character sketches**?

1.7.5. Can you use the subdivision --**Characters** under individual literary authors? *[Hint: see scope note under Characters and characteristics in literature.]*

1.7.6. Are you given a limitation for the use of **Métis**?

1.7.7. What is the difference between **Olympics** and **Olympic Games (21st : 1976 : Montréal, Québec)**?

1.7.8. Can --**Liturgy** be used as a subheading under **Baptists**? *[Hint: see scope note under Rites and ceremonies.]*

1.7.9. Can **Stencils and stencil cutting** be used as a subject heading for a book on the design of stencils for craft work?

1.8. *Subject Cataloging Manual: Subject Headings* and *Free-Floating Subdivisions: An Alphabetical Index*

The free-floating subdivisions used with *LCSH* appear in a number of different lists, each pertaining to a different subject category. These categories appear in the *Subject Cataloging Manual: Subject Headings* (5th edition, 1996), a marvelous tool issued by the Cataloging Policy and Support Office at the Library of Congress. The *Free-Floating Subdivisions: An Alphabetical Index* (9th ed., 1997) is an index to the *Subject Cataloging Manual*, with all free-floating subdivisions in the thirty-five separate categories indexed in one alphabetical sequence. The *Index* gives the term, the numbered list (H1095–H1200) in the *SCM:SH* from which it is taken, the named category from which it is taken, and any usage guidelines that may apply. The *Index* should be used only in conjunction with the *Manual*, as the term may have specific restrictions on its usage. These restrictions are to be found in footnotes or scope notes in the *Manual*, and do not appear in the *Index*. A key to the terms used under "Category" is given immediately preceding the list of subdivisions in the *Index*.

1.8. Subject Cataloging Manual

The fifth edition of the *Subject Cataloging Manual* is issued in four volumes. Volume 1 gives general introductory information such as assigning, changing, and proposing headings; citing sources; qualifiers; and more. Volume 2 contains information on subdivisions in general, subdivisions with dates, and multiple subdivisions, then continues with general information on free-floating subdivisions. The remainder of volume 2 consists of the categories and their lists of free-floating subdivisions, and background, explanatory, and cautionary notes. Volumes 3 and 4 contain special topics, materials, subdivisions, etc., from abstracts to yearbooks. Volume 4 also includes a glossary of abbreviations, capitalization, diacritics and special characters, and punctuation. Each separate section also gives a paragraph on LC practice within the category.

Read H 40 ("The Library of Congress Subject Authority File"), H 80 ("The Order of Subject Headings"), H 362 ("Free-Floating Terms and Phrases"), H 400 ("Scope Notes"), and H 1146 ("Subdivisions Controlled by Pattern Headings"). These will help you with the following exercises.

Subject Cataloging Manual and *Free-Floating Subdivisions* Exercises

Use the 5th edition (1996) of the *Subject Cataloging Manual: Subject Headings* and the 9th edition (1997) of the *Free-Floating Subdivisions: An Alphabetical Index* to complete these exercises.

1.8.1. Why do some of the subdivisions in the *Index* have a diamond shape preceding the given term?

1.8.2. Which categories allow you to subdivide by --**Interviews**?

1.8.3. Can --**Education** be qualified by level of instruction?

1.8.4. Can --**Officers' handbooks** be used as a subdivision under **Clubs**?

1.8.5. Can you tell this by reading *Free-Floating Subdivisions: An Alphabetical Guide*?

1.8.6. Why, or why not?

1.8.7. Are any free-floating subdivisions used under the main heading in *LCSH*?

1.8.8. Can you use --**Protestant churches** as a subdivision under **World War, 1914–1918**?

1.8.9. List the three form subdivisions dealing with statistics.

1.8.10. How are form subdivisions noted in the *Manual* and the *Index*?

1.8.11. If I want to know all the categories in which I can use the subdivision --**Genealogy**, where should I look?

1.8.12. Can --**Dialects** be used as a subdivision under individual literary authors?

1.8.13. Is there a subdivision under **Plants and crops** to cover field experiments?

1.8.14. Are there scope notes under all subdivisions in Volume 2?

1.8.15. Are you given *See* and *See Also* notes in the individual categories of free-floating subdivisions?

1.8.16. You are given two explanatory notes in H 1145.5 ("Free-Floating Subdivisions: Bodies of Water"). What are they about?

1.8.17. Does the definition given in H 1250 help distinguish the Library of Congress's use of these art terms?

1.8.18. Where would you find information on assigning subject headings for individual battles?

1.8.19. How many different types of civilization are discussed in H 1370? Name them.

1.8.20. How can you subdivide civilizations of particular places?

1.8.21. When did MARC coding of types of events change? *[Hint: see H 1592.]*

1.8.22. Give the four characteristics of events that are to be established in the name authority file and tagged as 111.

1.8.23. Do the instructions in H 1690 apply to the Annotated Card Program?

1.8.24. The subdivision --**Juvenile literature** may be assigned to textbooks for children through which grade and age level?

1.8.25. Materials of interest to genealogists and local historians would need a special subject heading of the type [place]-[topic]. Which section would you go to for instructions on assigning such a heading?

1.8.26. How many types of parks are included in the instructions in section H 1925?

1.8.27. How much of a work should be pictorial in nature to warrant the use of --**Pictorial works** as a subdivision?

1.8.28. Can you use --**Public opinion** as a subdivision for **Albuquerque (N.M.)**?

1.8.29. When can you assign a subject heading for a named computer program?

1.8.30. How many levels of education can be used as qualifiers to --**Study and teaching**? Name the qualifiers.

1.8.31. Where is the glossary found in the *Subject Cataloging Manual: Subject Headings*?

1.8.32. Does the section of the appendix dealing with Abbreviations give you a list of abbreviations that may be used?

1.8.33. Where would you find instructions on spacing in headings?

1.8.34. Is there an index to the *Subject Cataloging Manual: Subject Headings*?

1.8.35. Does it duplicate the *Free-Floating Subdivisions: An Index*?

1.9. Subdivisions on History

Read H 1647 in the *Subject Cataloging Manual: Subject Headings*. This gives specific information and restrictions on the use of --**History** as a subdivision within the *Library of Congress Subject Headings*.

The general rule is that --**History** may be used in most cases for descriptions and explanations of past events concerning the topic, group, sacred work, place, or organization. There are, however, certain conditions under which you cannot use the subdivision; for example, topics for which a specific phrase heading has been established, such as **Church history**; historical source material, such as **China--Foreign relations--Sources**; topical subdivisions that are explicitly or implicitly historical, such as **Military history, Modern--20th century**; or inverted headings beginning with the word **Philosophy**, such as **Philosophy, French--18th century**.

Most countries have established chronological subdivisions under the subdivision --**History**. These may be used as they are established within the *LCSH* volumes. An exercise in using these chronological subdivisions follows.

LCSH History Subdivisions Exercises

You are cataloging a collection of books dealing with history. Give the appropriate geographic subject heading, with history subdivisions, for each. If there is another appropriate subject heading, give it also. Use appropriate MARC tagging.

1.9.1. An account of the Battle of Teutoburger Wald.

1.9.2. Ch'in dynasty humor.

1.9.3. Life in the colonies of the United States in the 17th century.

1.9.4. A treatise on the Battle of Lake Champlain in 1609.

1.9.5. A history of life in France under the Carolingians.

1.9.6. A history of the Greek battle of Issus in 333 B.C.

1.9.7. The life and times of Otto IV, ruler of Germany in the early 13th century.

1.9.8. A treatise on the Latin empire in France in the 13th century.

1.9.9. A history of the six dynasties of China, from the third to the sixth centuries.

1.9.10. A child's book about life in Canada in the 19th century.

1.9.11. Life during the Age of Pericles.

1.9.12. Biographies of soldiers, both British and American, who fought in King William's War.

1.9.13. Refugees from the German revolution of 1848.

1.9.14. Casualties in the French and Indian War.

1.9.15. Life and times of the common people of the Chinese T'ang dynasty.

1.9.16. A history of the Confederation of Canada, 1867.

1.9.17. Greek war of independence during the 1820s.

1.9.18. Censorship during the French revolution of the 1790s.

1.9.19. Posters from the German revolution of 1918.

1.9.20. A child's book about the French Reign of Terror.

1.9.21. A book about the campaigns of the Canadian rebellion of 1837.

1.9.22. A juvenile book on the battlefields of the American Revolution.

1.9.23. Life in the five dynasties and ten kingdoms of China in the 10th century.

1.9.24. A bibliography of works about the German reunification of 1990.

1.9.25. Life in medieval Greece.

1.9.26. Historiography of the Chinese Ming dynasty.

1.9.27. Canadian spy trials in the 1940s.

1.9.28. Life in France during the February Revolution.

1.9.29. A bibliography on the Greek revolution of 1848.

1.9.30. A novel about the Burr-Hamilton duel of 1804.

1.9.31. A textbook on the military history of Germany in the 19th century.

1.9.32. Pictorial work about the Cultural Revolution in China.

1.9.33. A bibliography on the Fifth French Republic.

1.9.34. Anecdotes from American naval history.

1.9.35. A child's book about the 1950s history of Greece.

1.10. Biography Subdivisions

Read sections H 1330, H 1480, H 1538, and H 1678 in the *Subject Cataloging Manual: Subject Headings*. They give general and specific instructions on assigning biographical subdivisions and distinguishing biographical as opposed to critical works on the individual's professional, intellectual, or artistic achievements. Also included is information on such materials as correspondence, diaries, and interviews.

To apply the subdivision --**Biography**, a work must devote more than 50% of its content to the personal aspects of the life of one or more individuals. It also should cover a relatively large portion of the individual's life, not just a single brief incident. A partial biography includes some, but less than 50%, biographical material.

Also read sections H 1110 and H 1155.4 in *SCM:SH*. These sections deal with subdivisions for individuals in general and for individual literary authors. **Shakespeare, William, 1564-1616** serves as the pattern heading for literary authors.

Use the information in *SCM:SH* to answer the following questions on assigning subdivisions to works of biography and autobiography.

1.10.1. Does the definition of "personal aspects" apply to historical figures from the distant past? Why or why not?

1.10. Biography Subdivisions   31

1.10.2.   When cataloging a work of correspondence, how many personal name headings would you use?

1.10.3.   If there are more than three letter writers included, how many names do you include in the subject headings?

1.10.4.   Under which topics is --**Interviews** used as a subdivision?

1.10.5.   What other aspects of a work are included in the subject headings of a biography besides the name of the biographee?

1.10.6.   Why would you assign a "class of persons" heading to a biography?

1.10.7.   How many individuals who receive correspondence would you assign subject headings for?

1.10.8.   Can **Interviews** be used as a heading as well as a subdivision?

1.10.9.   For biographees with multifaceted lives or careers, do you assign only one heading that best encompasses the career or lifelong pursuits, or would you assign more than one? Why?

1.10.10. Would you assign "class of persons" headings, or ethnic group headings, if the writer (not the addressee) can be identified with a particular discipline or group?

1.10.11. If a name has been established in *LCSH* and has its own subdivisions, can you use the free-floating list as established in *SCM:SH*, section H 1110?

1.10.12. Would you routinely assign headings that specify the sex or ethnic group of the class of persons to which the biographee belongs?

1.10.13. Could you add the subdivision --**Sources** or --**History--Sources** to a collection of correspondence?

1.10.14. Can you create specific topics as subdivisions under names of persons who are not prominent or well known if they are already created under the name of a famous person in *LCSH*?

1.10.15. Would you ever assign a heading only to a topic rather than to a class of persons, place, or event?

1.10.16. When would you assign headings of the type **English letters** or **German letters** to a collection of personal letters?

1.10.17. Would you assign personal name headings for the writers of the collection in question #1.10.16?

1.10.18. If there is a conflict between subdivisions in the general persons list (section H 1110) and the literary authors list (section H 1155.4), which takes precedence?

1.10.19. When would you assign headings for place, organization, or event in cataloging a biographical work?

1.10.20. Give the definition of **Diaries** from the *SCM:SH*.

1.10.21. Does the list of free-floating subdivisions given in section H 1110 include form subdivisions?

1.10.22. Would you assign a "class of persons" heading to the founder of a major religion?

1.10.23. How many and what type of subject headings would you use when cataloging a diary?

1.10.24. Do you use section H 1155.4 of the *SCM:SH* for groups of literary authors?

1.10.25. Which part of *SCM:SH* would you use for groups of literary authors?

1.10.26. Would you ever assign the subdivision --**Biography** to a book about an animal?

1.10.27. Which section in *SCM:SH* tells you this?

1.10.28. What is the subdivision you would use with the name of a diarist?

1.10.29. Does the pattern heading for literary authors include subdivisions not applicable to Shakespeare? Why or why not?

1.10.30. Are any special headings assigned to biographies of immigrants?

1.10.31. Where do you find the information referred to in question #1.10.30?

1.10.32. When a single diary is being cataloged, would you assign both a "class of persons" heading and an ethnic group heading? If not, which one would be preferred?

1.10.33. Does the list of free-floating subdivisions in section H 1155.4 give cross-references?

1.10.34. What type of biography contains more about the history of the time than the life of the biographee?

1.10.35. Is there a separate list of free-floating subdivisions for literary works entered under title?

1.10.36. You are cataloging a biography of Barbara Bush. How many subject headings will you need? List them.

1.10.37. You are cataloging a collective biography of the immediate family of President Kennedy immediately after his death. How many subject headings will you need? List them.

1.10.38. You are cataloging a biography of football coach Bear Bryant. How many subject headings will you use? List them.

1.10.39. You are cataloging a collective biography of the wives of Henry VIII. How many subject headings will you use? List them.

1.10.40. You are cataloging a collection of letters by great French Renaissance literary authors. How many subject headings will you use? List them.

1.10.41. You are cataloging a collection of letters written during the Korean War by Cajun men to their wives in Louisiana. How many subject headings will you use? List them.

1.10.42. You are cataloging a collection of letters from Colonel Sam Pickering to his son, Tom Pickering, concerning the breeding of his racehorses in Virginia. How many subject headings will you assign? List them.

1.10.43. You are cataloging a set of diaries written by American pioneers who traveled the Oregon Trail. How many subject headings will you assign? List them.

1.11. Bible Headings and Subdivisions

Works about the Bible, the Bible itself, and subdivisions for this sacred work can be difficult for a cataloger to handle. It helps to remember that **Bible** is the *title* of the work, and therefore is always coded as a title—main title, uniform title, uniform title subject heading, or uniform title added entry.

Bible is the pattern heading for sacred works such as *The Book of Mormon, Koran, Tipitaka,* and *Vedas*. Any heading listed under **Bible** can be used with other sacred works.

There are several areas of the *Subject Cataloging Manual: Subject Headings* which cover the Bible. Assignment of subject headings about the Bible is covered in section H 1295. Information on commentaries is found in section H 1435 (3). Establishing [topic] **in the Bible** headings can be found in section H 1295 (1), and information about versions or translations is in section H 1300. The free-floating subdivisions are listed in H 1188. Read all these sections in *SCM:SH* for assistance in completing the following exercise.

1.11.1. What types of books about the Bible are found in Section H 1295?

1.11.2. How does *SCM:SH* define *versions*?

1.11.3. How does *SCM:SH* define *commentary*?

1.11.4. Can the subdivisions found in H 1188 be used under individual parts of the Bible as well as the Bible as a whole?

1.11.5. What subdivision would you use for the process of rendering a book from one language to another, including the methodology and tools?

1.11.6. What subdivision would you use for a commentary on the Koran?

1.11.7. Would you use **Bible--[subdivision]** or **[topic] in the Bible** for works on special topics discussed in the Bible?

1.11.8. What subdivision would you use for a general work dealing with various translations of a sacred work or one of its parts?

1.11.9. Are apocryphal works covered by the pattern heading **Bible**?

1.11.10. Can you use **Bible--Theology** or **Bible--Ethics** for theological or ethical teachings of the Bible or its parts?

1.11.11. When would you use the subdivision --**Versions, Slavic**?

1.11. Bible Headings and Subdivisions

1.11.12. How would you designate a Nepalese version of the Bible?

1.11.13. How would you designate a Nepalese version of the Bible intended for Lutherans?

1.11.14. When can you use the subdivision --**Criticism, interpretation, etc., Jewish**?

1.11.15. What subdivision would you use for religious or secular subject headings when the work being cataloged contains theological or ethical teachings of the Bible or its parts?

1.11.16. When can you use the subdivision --**Quotations in the New Testament**?

1.11.17. When can you use the subdivision --**Relation to the Old Testament**?

1.11.18. You are cataloging a work about salvation in the Gospel of Mark. How many subject headings would you use? List them.

1.11.19. You are cataloging a work about parenting emphasizing an environment based on Biblical teachings. How many subject headings would you use? List them.

1.11.20. You are cataloging a work about clothing worn by the Disciples. How many subject headings would you use? List them.

1.11.21. You are cataloging a bibliography of scriptures in Chinese languages. How many subject headings would you use? List them.

1.12. Special Subdivisions from *SCM:SH*

Read from *Subject Cataloging Manual: Subject Headings* sections H 1935 (Pictorial works), H 1592 (Events), H 1627 (Folklore), H 1845 (Local history), H 1955 (Public opinion), H 1997 (Religion), and 1998 (Religious aspects). Use the instructions to help you with the following exercises.

1.12.1. What type of work is usually cataloged with the subdivision --**Pictorial works**?

1.12.2. How is *event* defined by *SCM:SH*?

1.12.3. Can you assign a place name without a subdivision, even though it would be of use to local historians?

1.12.4. Can you use --**Public opinion** directly under the name of a place?

1.12.5. How much of a volume must consist of pictures before the subdivision --**Pictorial works** can be used?

1.12.6. Can you use the subdivision --**Pictorial works** if less than 50% of the work is pictures?

1.12.7. How many categories of events are established as subject headings? Name the first and last headings given.

1.12.8. How many categories of events are established as name headings? Name the first and last headings given.

1.12. Special Subdivisions from SCM:SH   39

1.12.9.   How many free-floating subdivisions could be added to a place name to subdivide it by topic? Give the first three.

1.12.10. What do you use if none of the specific subdivisions is appropriate?

1.12.11. What subdivision do you use to designate foreign opinion about regions or countries?

1.12.12. Can you use --**Foreign public opinion** under names of cities or counties?

1.12.13. The subdivision --**Pictorial works** replaced two other headings. What were the former headings for this type of work?

1.12.14. For events created in phrase forms, what three elements should be present?

1.12.15. Do you include the date in all cases?

1.12.16. What materials would have the subject heading [place]--Genealogy?

1.12.17. Can you subdivide --**Religion** by --**History**?

1.12.18. What subdivision would you use for a work stressing the visual identity of a group of people?

1.12.19. Can events be used as a subdivision under a corporate name?

1.12.20. Would you ever use a subject heading for a country subdivided by --**Genealogy**?

1.12.21. Can you subdivide --**Religion** chronologically?

1.12.22. Where would you go to find instructions on the use of --**Illustrations**?

1.12.23. How does *SCM:SH* define *folklore*?

1.12.24. Would --**History, Local** be appropriate as a subdivision for all places?

1.12.25. Can individual religions be subdivided geographically, or is the place subdivided by the individual religion?

1.12.26. Would you use --**Pictorial works** for atlases?

1.12.27. Can **Folklore** be used as a heading as well as a subheading?

1.12.28. How many types of subjects are listed in H 1845 as being of interest to historians? List the types.

1.12.29. Can you use the subdivision --**Religion** under the names of individual persons?

1.12. Special Subdivisions from *SCM:SH* 41

1.12.30. Can you use the subdivision --**Religion** under the names of individual theologians?

1.12.31. Is --**Pictorial works** a topical subdivision or a form subdivision?

1.12.32. If you are cataloging a work of folklore of a specific Indian tribe, do you assign both the specific tribe's name and **Indians of North America** with the subdivision --**Folklore**?

1.12.33. Under what topics would --**Religious aspects** be used?

1.12.34. Would you assign the subheading --**Biography** or --**History, Local** to a work including biographical sketches of historical figures of my birthplace?

1.12.35. When would you use the subdivision --**Photographs**?

1.12.36. Can you use the subdivision --**Legends** with American Indian tribes?

1.12.37. How does *SCM:SH* define *public opinion*?

1.12.38. Can you use the subdivision --**Religious aspects** under classes of persons or ethnic groups?

1.12.39. Can you use the subdivision --**Folklore** under the headings for mythical beings such as ghosts or mermaids?

1.12.40. Can **Public opinion** be used as a heading as well as a subdivision?

1.12.41. Under what type of materials would you use the subdivision --**Mythology**?

1.12.42. What is the difference between **Fairy tales** and **Legends**?

1.12.43. How would **Tales** be used?

1.12.44. What subdivision would you use for the opinion held by a particular class of persons or ethnic group? (The subject heading is the class of persons or the ethnic group.)

1.12.45. How would you use --**Moral and ethical aspects** as a subdivision?

2.
SEARS LIST OF SUBJECT HEADINGS

Sears List of Subject Headings, usually just called *Sears*, is a controlled vocabulary listing of subject headings, originally prepared in 1923 by Minnie Earl Sears and designed to meet the needs of small libraries. It is still used by many public and school libraries and is currently in its 16th edition, edited by Joseph Miller.

All headings that may be used as subject headings are printed in bold type, whether in the main file, in a *See Also* paragraph, in a *Use For* reference, or as an example. If a term is not printed in bold type, it cannot be used as a heading.

Sears, like *LCSH*, gives specific headings for use in libraries. Unlike *LCSH*, *Sears* allows the cataloger to create headings in certain situations. Read page xxxix in the 16th edition for instructions on adding specific headings. *Sears* also provides key headings (*LCSH* calls them pattern headings) whose subdivisions may be used under other headings of the same type. See the list in *Sears* on page xl.

A section on form or topical headings is given in *Sears* on page xviii. You may use these commonly used subdivisions under subjects as needed. These subdivisions are also called free-floating subdivisions. Subdivisions listed under the key headings are not included in this list.

Sears List of Subject Headings uses the same terminology as *LCSH*: UF [*Use For*], SA [*See Also*], BT [*Broader Term*], NT [*Narrower Term*], and RT [*Related Term*]. Unlike *LCSH*, *Sears* also gives associated Dewey Decimal classification numbers with the main headings. Sometimes a single number may be suggested (Cyclones 551.55) and other times a range of numbers is suggested (Death 128; 236; 306.9; 571.9), giving you options as to where the book could be placed for optimum use by patrons and reference librarians.

Read the "Preface," pages vii–xi, and "Principles of the *Sears List of Subject Headings*," pages xv–xxxviii in the 16th edition.

2.1. *Sears* Subject Heading Exercises

Give three subject headings for each topic below. When cataloging the book in a work situation you might use less than three, but as *Sears* prohibits the use of more than three, and for the purpose of these exercises, construct three subject headings. You may wish to use the "List of Commonly Used Subdivisions" on pages xli–xliii in the 16th edition of *Sears List of Subject Headings*.

44 *Sears List of Subject Headings*

2.1.1. A biography of Huey Long.

   A. _____

   B. _____

   C. _____

2.1.2. A history of the Louisiana State Department of Education from 1850 to 1950.

   A. _____

   B. _____

   C. _____

2.1.3. Tunica-Biloxi Indian tribal customs.

   A. _____

   B. _____

   C. _____

2.1.4. Black soldiers who took part in the Civil War.

   A. _____

   B. _____

   C. _____

2.1.5. Plantations and plantation life in New Orleans.

   A. _____

   B. _____

   C. _____

2.1.6. Oil leases in the Gulf of Mexico.

   A. _____

   B. _____

   C. _____

2.1.7. Prize-winning library buildings in Louisiana.

    A. _____

    B. _____

    C. _____

2.1.8. A genealogy of the Hebert family of New Orleans.

    A. _____

    B. _____

    C. _____

2.1.9. Legal status of hazardous waste disposal in salt domes.

    A. _____

    B. _____

    C. _____

2.1.10. Public hearing for a road project in Cobb County, Georgia.

    A. _____

    B. _____

    C. _____

2.1.11. Flood damage reduction project in Johnstown, Pennsylvania.

    A. _____

    B. _____

    C. _____

2.1.12. Schools and school attendance in Louisiana's Florida Parishes in the 18th century.

    A. _____

    B. _____

    C. _____

2.1.13. History of Arpadhon, a Hungarian settlement in southeast Louisiana.

   A. _____

   B. _____

   C. _____

2.1.14. Political situation in Sarajevo.

   A. _____

   B. _____

   C. _____

2.1.15. Troop movements in Operation Desert Storm.

   A. _____

   B. _____

   C. _____

2.1.16. Printing presses in 18th-century Germany.

   A. _____

   B. _____

   C. _____

2.1.17. Case studies of persons with AIDS.

   A. _____

   B. _____

   C. _____

2.1.18. Debate on euthanasia.

   A. _____

   B. _____

   C. _____

2.1. Sears Subject Heading Exercises

2.1.19. A history of the Great Wall of China.

    A. _____

    B. _____

    C. _____

2.1.20. A biography of Richard Nixon.

    A. _____

    B. _____

    C. _____

2.1.21. Plantation life in the area around Richmond, Virginia.

    A. _____

    B. _____

    C. _____

2.1.22. A history of the Missoula, Montana, Mayor's Office.

    A. _____

    B. _____

    C. _____

2.1.23. Cherokee Indian marriage customs.

    A. _____

    B. _____

    C. _____

2.1.24. A list of veterans from Alabama who fought in the Civil War.

    A. _____

    B. _____

    C. _____

2.1.25. Alaskan pipelines and their construction and maintenance.

　　A. _____

　　B. _____

　　C. _____

2.1.26. Encyclopedia of Louisiana irises.

　　A. _____

　　B. _____

　　C. _____

2.1.27. Legal issues in junk bond trading.

　　A. _____

　　B. _____

　　C. _____

2.1.28. A genealogy of the Whitefield family of Shawnee, Kansas.

　　A. _____

　　B. _____

　　C. _____

2.1.29. Damage by Hurricane Andrew in Florida and Louisiana.

　　A. _____

　　B. _____

　　C. _____

2.1.30. Freight traffic on the Erie Canal during the 19th century.

　　A. _____

　　B. _____

　　C. _____

2.1. Sears Subject Heading Exercises 49

2.1.31. Relationships between the Isletos and the settlers in New Mexico.

   A. _____

   B. _____

   C. _____

2.1.32. Public hearing for a proposed new Mississippi River bridge at St. Louis, Missouri.

   A. _____

   B. _____

   C. _____

2.1.33. Repair of all-terrain vehicles, particularly dune buggies and snowmobiles.

   A. _____

   B. _____

   C. _____

2.1.34. Mount Everest climbing expeditions.

   A. _____

   B. _____

   C. _____

2.1.35. A biography of Anthony Panizzi.

   A. _____

   B. _____

   C. _____

2.1.36. Design and construction of cupolas and other decorative roof details.

   A. _____

   B. _____

   C. _____

50 *Sears List of Subject Headings*

2.2. *Sears Subject Heading Terminology and Scope Notes*

Sears List of Subject Headings uses abbreviations to indicate other headings that might be used as well as, or in place of, the heading given in bold text. Read the section on page lii in the 16th edition of *Sears*, which defines these abbreviations. Many scope notes are also used in this list. Additional scope notes identifying headings that may be assigned to individual works of fiction, poetry, and drama have been included. Give the answers to the exercises in the space allowed.

2.2.1. List the narrower terms given under the heading **Antiquities**.

2.2.2. List the broader terms given under the heading **Highway engineering**.

2.2.3. List the terms that may not be used under the heading **Motion pictures**.

2.2.4. List all the terms that you may use under the heading **Sea power**.

2.2.5. Give the former heading for **Linear algebra**.

2.2.6. Give the later headings for **Bicycles and bicycling**.

2.2.7. Can the heading **Academic freedom** be subdivided geographically?

2.2.8. May the heading **Lincoln family** be subdivided geographically?

2.2.9. May the heading **Passion plays** be subdivided geographically?

2.2. Sears Subject Heading Terminology and Scope Notes

2.2.10. Give the scope note for **Linguistics**.

2.2.11. List other headings that might also be used with **Berries**.

2.2.12. Are any other headings listed for use under **Lebanon**?

2.2.13. Are any subdivisions listed for use under **Germany**?

2.2.14. Can you use the subject heading **Musical films** for an individual film?

2.2.15. Can you use **Women in the motion picture industry** for a book dealing with the portrayal of women in motion pictures?

2.2.16. Can you use **Guerrilla warfare** for a book on military aspects of irregular warfare?

2.2.17. What other terms might I use for this subject?

2.2.18. What term must I use for a listing of movies shown on H.B.O.?

2.2.19. What term should I use for a book dealing with training of dogs for the blind?

2.2.20. Can you use **Rhetoric** as a heading for a composition in the French language?

2.2.21. What other subject heading might you use for the same item?

2.2.22. Can you use the subject heading in question #21 for a work in Japanese, by altering the name of the language?

2.2.23. How do you know the answer to question #22?

2.2.24. What level materials are used with the heading **Higher education**?

2.2.25. Do scope notes in *See Also* areas ever give specific headings you might wish to use?

2.2.26. What is a broader term for **National emblems**?

2.2.27. What is a related term for **National emblems**?

2.2.28. Can you use the heading **Native peoples** for a work on Australian aborigines?

2.2.29. Can you use the heading **Aborigines--Australia** for the work referred to in question #28?

2.2. Sears Subject Heading Terminology and Scope Notes 53

2.2.30. Give a related term for a work on industrial accidents.

2.2.31. Which subject headings would you use for a book containing the texts of various constitutions and their history?

2.2.32. *Sears List of Subject Headings* allows you to create headings of greater specificity. What tells you that a particular heading can be created?

2.2.33. What heading can you apply to a book on Judgment Day (the end of the world)?

2.2.34. What is the later heading that replaced **Chemistry, Inorganic**?

2.2.35. Give two broader terms for **Telemarketing**.

2.2.36. Can you use **Telephone directories** as a subdivision?

2.2.37. Can you use **Telephone directories** as a subject heading?

2.2.38. What is a broader term for **Quartz**?

2.2.39. What is a broader term for the answer to question #38?

2.3. *Sears* History Subdivisions

Read pages xxii–xxiii in *Sears List of Subject Headings* concerning the use of chronological subdivisions. As the current trend is to use dates rather than identifying names, *Sears*, unlike *LCSH*, has adopted the practice of always having dates precede phrases (--**1861-1865, Civil War**, as opposed to --**Civil War, 1861-1865** in *LCSH*). *Sears* is also a less complex list of headings; it includes chronological subdivisions only for those countries about whose history a small library is apt to acquire enough works that it would be useful to separate them into groups. The countries included are the United States, Great Britain, France, Germany, Italy, and a few others. The chronological subdivisions for these countries use broad ranges of dates rather than the finer, more detailed breakdowns found in *LCSH*.

Chronological subdivisions differ for each country. *Sears* does, however, allow libraries with larger than ordinary collections in the history of a particular country or region the option to establish period subdivisions and with them subdivide the material further than is spelled out in the *Sears* list.

Sears History Subdivisions Exercises

You are cataloging a collection of books dealing with history. Give the appropriate geographic subject heading, with history subdivisions, for each. Use appropriate MARC tagging.

2.3.1. An account of the Battle of Teutoburger Wald.

2.3.2. Ch'in dynasty humor.

2.3.3. Life in the colonies of the United States in the 17th century.

2.3.4. A treatise on the Battle of Lake Champlain in 1791.

2.3.5. A history of life in France under the Carolingians.

2.3.6. A history of the Greek battle of Issus in 333 B.C.

2.3.7. The life and times of Otto IV, ruler of Germany in the early 13th century.

2.3.8. A treatise on the Latin empire in France in the 13th century.

2.3.9. A history of the six dynasties of China, from the third to the sixth centuries.

2.3.10. A child's book about life in Canada in the 19th century.

2.3.11. Life during the Age of Pericles.

2.3.12. Biographies of soldiers, both British and American, who fought in King William's War.

2.3.13. Refugees from the German revolution of 1848.

2.3.14. Casualties in the French and Indian War.

2.3.15. Life and times of the common people of the Chinese T'ang dynasty.

2.3.16. A history of the Confederation of Canada in 1867.

2.3.17. Greek war of independence during the 1820s.

2.3.18. Censorship during the French revolution of the 1790s.

2.3.19. Posters from the German revolution of 1918.

2.3.20. A child's book about the French Reign of Terror.

2.3.21. A book about the campaigns of the Canadian rebellion of 1837.

2.3.22. A juvenile book on the battlefields of the American Revolution.

2.3.23. Life in the five dynasties and ten kingdoms of China in the 10th century.

2.3.24. A bibliography of works about the German reunification of 1990.

2.3.25. Life in medieval Greece.

2.3.26. Historiography of the Chinese Ming dynasty.

2.3.27. Canadian spy trials in the 1940s.

2.3.28. Life in France during the February Revolution.

2.3.29. A bibliography on the Greek revolution of 1848.

2.3.30. A novel about the Burr-Hamilton duel of 1804.

2.3.31. Pictorial work about the Cultural Revolution in China.

2.3.32. A bibliography on the Fifth French Republic.

2.3.33. Anecdotes from American naval history.

2.3.34. A child's book about the 1950s history of Greece.

3.
DEWEY DECIMAL CLASSIFICATION

Introduction

The Dewey Decimal classification system was devised by Melvil Dewey and first published in 1876. It divides the universe of knowledge into ten broad categories, or classes, which correspond to traditional academic disciplines. Each class is assigned a range of three-digit numbers (Religion 200–299) which is subdivided into divisions (Bible 220–229) and sections (New Testament 225). Each section can be further divided by the addition of decimal numbers for greater specificity (New Testament commentaries 225.7). Those aspects of the treatment of a subject that cross all boundaries, and are frequently used, have been organized into a table called Standard Subdivisions (Table 1). This corresponds to the free-floating subdivisions found in subject cataloging. The standard subdivisions include management, education and history, and publication types such as directories, dictionaries, indexes, and bibliographies. Sometimes these subdivisions are incorporated into the basic Dewey number in the schedules, and other times the schedule instructs you to add them to the number being assigned.

As knowledge grows and expands and new technologies appear, schedules become full and the numbers grow too long to be of use. When this happens, a schedule, or part of one, may be completely revised. This has happened most recently with the 780 (Music) schedule. Other areas that have been revised in the recent past include computers (001.6 changed to 004–006) and sociology (301).

The Dewey Decimal system is organized quite differently from the Library of Congress classification system. It is well suited to smaller libraries that do not need the specificity that larger collections require. Changing from one system to the other, however, can be a major project, and should not be undertaken lightly.

Dewey numbers can be created by using only the schedules and the index, by adding numbers to other numbers, or by adding numbers from the tables. The following exercises should help you become more comfortable with the Dewey Decimal classification and assign classification numbers more easily and accurately.

3.1. Dewey Relative Index Exercises

Use *DDC21*, volumes 1–4, to complete this exercise. You are given an author, a title, and a subject from the *Library of Congress Subject Headings* (*LCSH*). Using *DDC* volume 4, Index, look up the subject heading you have been given. Browse the suggested topics and numbers, and choose the one you think is the best suited to the title of the book. Check it in volumes 2 or 3 and write your answer on the line.

3.1.1. Author: Tulane Environmental Law Clinic.
Title: Citizen's guide to environmental activism in Louisiana.
LCSH: Environmental protection--Citizen participation.

Dewey: _____

3.1.2. Author: Louisiana Office of Historic Preservation.
Title: Bibliography of archaeological survey and mitigation reports: Louisiana.
LCSH: Louisiana--Antiquities--Bibliography.

Dewey: _____

3.1.3. Author: Cowen, David L.
Title: Pharmacy, an illustrated history.
LCSH: Pharmacy--History.

Dewey: _____

3.1.4. Author: Collins, Mark.
Title: The last rain forests.
LCSH: Rainforests.

Dewey: _____

3.1.5. Author: Martin, Ann.
Title: The secrets of showjumping success in competitions.
LCSH: Show jumping.

Dewey: _____

3.1.6. Author: Dittman, Margaret.
Title: How to make baby quilts.
LCSH: Quilting.

Dewey: _____

3.1.7. Author: Church, D.C.
Title: Livestock feeds and feeding.
LCSH: Animal nutrition.

Dewey: _____

3.1. Dewey Relative Index Exercises

3.1.8. Author: Stewart, Harry L.
Title: Pumps.
LCSH: Pumping machinery.

Dewey: _____

3.1.9. Author: Highsmith, Dewey.
Title: Barge traffic on the Intracoastal Canal.
LCSH: Gulf Intracoastal Canal.

Dewey: _____

3.1.10. Author: Hope, Fuller.
Title: Freeze for the future: or, The technology of cryogenics.
LCSH: Low temperature engineering.

Dewey: _____

3.1.11. Author: Cajan, Ima.
Title: Transportation on Bayou Lafourche.
LCSH: Bayous--Louisiana

Dewey: _____

3.1.12. Author: Smith, Adam R.
Title: Greece during the early Byzantine Empire after 500 A.D.
LCSH: Greece--History--323-1453.

Dewey: _____

3.1.13. Author: Stephanopoulos, Demetrius Constantine.
Title: Studies in the Imperial sculpture of the Eastern Byzantine Empire, 1044-1150.
LCSH: Sculpture, Byzantine.

Dewey: _____

3.1.14. Author: Tweed, Digby.
Title: How to get rid of weeds in your flower garden.
LCSH: Weeds.

Dewey: _____

3.1.15. Author: Pringle, Dolly.
Title: How to make beanbags.
LCSH: Soft toys.

Dewey: _____

62 *Dewey Decimal Classification*

    3.1.16. Author: Drinkman, Ivanna.
            Title: Drink and driving: substance abuse as a cause of motorcycle accidents.
            LCSH: Drinking and traffic accidents.

    Dewey: _____

3.2. Dewey Schedules Exercises

Use the *DDC21* index (volume 4) to find numbers where these books would be classified. Then check them in volumes 2–3. The items are grouped by subject. Write the Dewey number on the blank.

    3.2.1.   A general cookbook. _____

    3.2.2.   A book on cooking for beginners. _____

    3.2.3.   A book on cooking for the Christmas holidays. _____

    3.2.4.   A book on cooking in mass quantities, e.g., for hotels. _____

    3.2.5.   A book on Cajun (Louisiana) cooking. _____

    3.2.6.   A book on gumbo recipes. _____

    3.2.7.   A book on making strawberry jam. _____

    3.2.8.   A book on making punch. _____

    3.2.9.   A book on cake decorating. _____

    3.2.10. A book on low-fat cookery. _____

    3.2.11. A book on comparative religion. _____

    3.2.12. A book on Christianity. _____

3.2.13. A biography of Jesus Christ. _____

3.2.14. A book on creation versus evolution. _____

3.2.15. A commentary on the Gospel of St. Luke. _____

3.2.16. A book on evangelism. _____

3.2.17. A book of sermons for children. _____

3.2.18. A book on Gothic art in churches. _____

3.2.19. A book on saints. _____

3.2.20. A book on the history of Judaism. _____

3.2.21. A book on recreation centers. _____

3.2.22. A book on circuses. _____

3.2.23. An encyclopedia of motion pictures. _____

3.2.24. A book on monster films. _____

3.2.25. A collection of film reviews. _____

3.2.26. A book on how to play chess. _____

3.2.27. A history of American football. _____

3.2.28. A book on canoeing. _____

64 *Dewey Decimal Classification*

3.2.29. A manual for spearfishing. _____

3.2.30. A book on big game hunting. _____

3.2.31. A book about automobiles. _____

3.2.32. A book about maintenance of automobiles. _____

3.2.33. A book about off-road vehicles. _____

3.2.34. A book about automobile racing. _____

3.2.35. A book on taking photographs of automobiles. _____

3.2.36. A book about mobile home camping. _____

3.2.37. A book about automobile accidents. _____

3.2.38. A book about vehicle product liability. _____

3.2.39. A book about regulation and control of taxis. _____

3.2.40. A book about raising horses. _____

3.2.41. A book about horseshoeing. _____

3.2.42. A book about horse racing. _____

3.2.43. A book about horse flies. _____

3.2.44. A book about the use of horses in the military. _____

3.2. Dewey Schedules Exercises

3.2.45. A book about streetcars that are pulled by horses. _____

3.2.46. A book on the manufacture of equipment for equestrian sports. _____

3.2.47. A book about polo. _____

3.2.48. A book of photographs of horses. _____

3.2.49. A book on how to get rid of dead horses. _____

3.2.50. A book about boats. _____

3.2.51. A book about the design and construction of sailboats. _____

3.2.52. A book about the maintenance of outboard motors. _____

3.2.53. A collection of drawings of boats. _____

3.2.54. A book on the joys of yachting. _____

3.2.55. A book on the legal aspects of salvage operations. _____

3.2.56. A book on boating safety. _____

3.2.57. A manual for the Coast Guard harbor patrol. _____

3.2.58. A book on navigation by sonar. _____

3.2.59. A book on ferry boat services. _____

3.2.60. A manual on rigging safety equipment in ships. _____

66 *Dewey Decimal Classification*

3.3. Number Building from Schedules

Read the section on number building in the introduction to *DDC21*, pages xlv–xlviii (8.1–8.20). The following exercise will demonstrate how part c (8.16 and 8.17, pages xlvii–xlviii) is used to create a new number by adding from other parts of the schedules.

Dewey numbers are constructed using three digits followed by a decimal. The numbers following the decimal further limit the concept being classified. All Dewey numbers have a minimum of three digits, and none can have more than one decimal. When creating new numbers using the number-building technique, first create your final number, then insert the decimal at the proper place.

Paragraph 8.16 instructs you to make a direct addition to a number from another part of the schedule, that is, to add to the base number notation 001–999. This means that you are to add ANY section of the schedules to the base number. For instance, 025.06 (Information storage and retrieval systems devoted to specific disciplines and subjects) includes a section on specific disciplines and subjects. It tells you to add to base number 025.06 notation 001–999. If you wanted to create a call number for MEDLINE, you would add the Dewey number for medicine, the specific discipline for the database. No Dewey number can end in a zero, therefore you must drop the final zero, leaving only the two digits to be added. The easiest way to do this is to use the chart below.

    Base number   __025.06__

    Full number from which a part will be taken   __610__

    Numbers to be added   __61__

    Final call number   __025.0661__

In 8.17 you are instructed to use only part of another number. The basic idea is the same, but you must delete more of the suggested Dewey number to be added. If, for example, you are cataloging a book about services to persons with rheumatoid arthritis, you would go to 362.149 and follow the directions given in the schedules. Using the chart, you would proceed as follows:

    Base number   __362.19__

    Full number from which a part will be taken   __616.7227__

    Numbers to be added   __67227__

    Final call number   __362.1967227__

To create the final call number, append the numbers from the third line to the base number, and put your decimal after the third digit from the left. Use the charts given with each of the following exercises to construct a new call number.

3.3. Number Building from Schedules   67

Number Building Exercises

3.3.1. A book about the photography of animals.

Base number _____

Full number from which a part will be taken _____

Numbers to be added _____

Final call number _____

3.3.2. History of transportation by clipper ships.

Base number _____

Full number from which a part will be taken _____

Numbers to be added _____

Final call number _____

3.3.3. How-to manual for a computerized football game. *[Hint: this is a computer game!]*

Base number _____

Full number from which a part will be taken _____

Numbers to be added _____

Final call number _____

3.3.4. A history of Catholic missions.

Base number _____

Full number from which a part will be taken _____

Numbers to be added _____

Final call number _____

3.3.5. Economic aspects of operating a seaplane service. *[Hint: start with 387.]*

Base number _____

Full number from which a part will be taken _____

Numbers to be added _____

Final call number _____

68 *Dewey Decimal Classification*

3.3.6. Control of leaf beetles in maple forests.

    Base number _____

    Full number from which a part will be taken _____

    Numbers to be added _____

    Final call number _____

3.3.7. Explanation of planetary rings, particularly around Saturn. *[Hint: don't start with Saturn!]*

    Base number _____

    Full number from which a part will be taken _____

    Numbers to be added _____

    Final call number _____

3.3.8. A book about military flame-throwers.

    Base number _____

    Full number from which a part will be taken _____

    Numbers to be added _____

    Final call number _____

3.3.9. A book about miniature tractors.

    Base number _____

    Full number from which a part will be taken _____

    Numbers to be added _____

    Final call number _____

3.3.10. A book about how to draw loons.

    Base number _____

    Full number from which a part will be taken _____

    Numbers to be added _____

    Final call number _____

3.3.11. A collection of Presbyterian prayers.

　　　Base number _____

　　　Full number from which a part will be taken _____

　　　Numbers to be added _____

　　　Final call number _____

3.3.12. A book about heart development in human fetuses.

　　　Base number _____

　　　Full number from which a part will be taken _____

　　　Numbers to be added _____

　　　Final call number _____

3.3.13. A book about aptitude tests for gifted pianists.

　　　Base number _____

　　　Full number from which a part will be taken _____

　　　Numbers to be added _____

　　　Final call number _____

3.3.14. A book about prospecting for manganese.

　　　Base number _____

　　　Full number from which a part will be taken _____

　　　Numbers to be added _____

　　　Final call number _____

3.3.15. A book about the shortage of sulphur resources in the United States. *[Hint: try Mineral resources.]*

　　　Base number _____

　　　Full number from which a part will be taken _____

　　　Numbers to be added _____

　　　Final call number _____

70 Dewey Decimal Classification

3.3.16. A book about bass fisheries.

   Base number _____

   Full number from which a part will be taken _____

   Numbers to be added _____

   Final call number _____

3.3.17. A treatise on Shinto schools in the United States.

   Base number _____

   Full number from which a part will be taken _____

   Numbers to be added _____

   Final call number _____

3.3.18. A book about forecasting ice storms.

   Base number _____

   Full number from which a part will be taken _____

   Numbers to be added _____

   Final call number _____

3.3.19. A book about the manufacture of shotguns and other hunting equipment.

   Base number _____

   Full number from which a part will be taken _____

   Numbers to be added _____

   Final call number _____

3.3.20. A bibliography of materials about oscilloscopes.

   Base number _____

   Full number from which a part will be taken _____

   Numbers to be added _____

   Final call number _____

3.4. Number Building from Tables

Read the section on number building in the introduction to *DDC21*, pages xlv–xlviii (8.1–8.20). This section teaches you how to build numbers using the tables in volume 1. Tables are indexed in volume 4, just as numbers in the schedules are indexed. Numbers from the Tables are preceded by a hyphen (-) and a letter "T" with the number of the table to which they belong, e.g., T5 -971|2 means that -971|2 stands for "Inuit" in Table 5.

Most catalogers become familiar with Tables 1 and 2 fairly quickly, but use Tables 3–7 much less often. These exercises contain examples from all seven tables.

Table 1 is also called Standard Subdivisions. These numbers allow you to specify the treatment of a book (bibliography, history, education) or to specify such information as language, genre, or type of person. Most standard subdivisions are preceded with a single zero. Sometimes, however, depending on the complexity of the schedule in question, the cataloger is instructed to add extra zeros (for standard subdivisions, use -0001 to -0009) or no zeros at all (for standard subdivisions, use -1 to -9).

For instance, if you were cataloging a book on interior decoration in the 1920s, you would go to 747.2049, and add numbers from Table 1, as instructed, to specify the time period.

Base number ___747.2049___

Notation from Table 1 ___-09042___

Numbers to be added ___2___

Final call number ___747.20492___

Table 2 contains information on geographic areas, historical periods, and persons. If you were cataloging a book on interior decoration in Mongolia, you would go to 747.2 and add as instructed to indicate the geographic area.

Base number ___747.2___

Notation from Table 2 ___-5173___

Full number to be added ___5173___

Final call number ___747.25173___

Table 2 numbers are often used to create call numbers for the history or geography of a place. History numbers are created by adding "9" before the Table 2 number, and geographical (or materials with current information) numbers are created by adding "91" to the Table 2 numbers. For example, for a history of Nepal, go to the index and find the Table 2 number (-5496) and add "9" to the front of it, in place of the "-". Add the decimal three digits from the left and your number is 954.96. For a travel guide to Nepal, add "91" to the beginning of the Table 2 number, add a decimal, and your classification is 915.496.

Table 3 contains information about works of literature. It is divided into three parts. Table 3-A contains subdivisions for works by or about individual authors; Table 3-B contains

72 *Dewey Decimal Classification*

subdivisions for works by or about more than one author; and Table 3-C contains notations to be added where instructed in Table 3-B, 700.4, 791.4, and 808–809. As you can see, use of Table 3-C is very limited.

Read page 406 in volume 1. It tells you to add the Table 3 number to the base number to create a specific classification. This introduction also tells you specific procedures for adding the numbers for chronological periods.

Read the introductions for Table 3-B and Table 3-C on pages 411–413 of volume 1. This Table is more complex than Table 3-A, and allows you to be more specific about the literatures involved. The numbers for Table 3-C are added to the numbers for Table 3-B. For example, to the notation in Table 3-B for a literary form (poetry, drama, fiction) will be appended notations from Table 3-C for specific periods, specific subjects, or specific features.

Table 4 gives the subdivisions of individual languages and language families, to be added according to the notes under specific languages (i.e., French) or language families (i.e., Romance languages). Read the explanation given on page 468 of volume 2 (420–490 Specific languages).

Table 5 delineates racial, ethnic, and national groups. Read the explanation given on pages 444–445 in volume 1.

Table 6 is used for translations or regions only where this use is specified in the schedules. It may never be used alone. Read the explanation given on page 464 in volume 1.

Table 7 is used for groups of persons. It is separated into groups by racial, ethnic, or national background; by sex and kinship; by age; by miscellaneous social characteristics; by physical and mental characteristics; and by occupations. It may be used only where noted in the schedules.

Number Building from Tables Exercises

Table 1

    3.4.1.   An encyclopedia of pottery.

        Base number _____

        Notation from Table 1 _____

        Numbers to be added _____

        Final call number _____

    3.4.2.   A book on treating waste products in a glass factory.

        Base number _____

        Notation from Table 1 _____

        Numbers to be added _____

        Final call number _____

3.4. Number Building from Tables 73

3.4.3. In-service training manual for naval personnel being sent to war. *[Hint: see note about adding standard subdivisions.]*

    Base number _____

    Notation from Table 1 _____

    Numbers to be added _____

    Final call number _____

3.4.4. Management of scenery in a theater.

    Base number _____

    Notation from Table 1 _____

    Numbers to be added _____

    Final call number _____

Table 2

3.4.5. A book on postal service in Tibet.

    Base number _____

    Notation from Table 2 _____

    Numbers to be added _____

    Final call number _____

3.4.6. A book about the library in West Baton Rouge Parish, Louisiana.

    Base number _____

    Notation from Table 2 _____

    Numbers to be added _____

    Final call number _____

3.4.7. A book about haunted homes in Westchester County, New York.

    Base number _____

    Notation from Table 2 _____

74 *Dewey Decimal Classification*

    Numbers to be added _____

    Final call number _____

3.4.8. A book about holy places in Canterbury, England.

    Base number _____

    Notation from Table 2 _____

    Numbers to be added _____

    Final call number _____

Table 3-A

3.4.9. French drama.

    Base number _____

    Notation from Table 3-A _____

    Numbers to be added _____

    Final call number _____

3.4.10. Spanish poetry.

    Base number _____

    Notation from Table 3-A _____

    Numbers to be added _____

    Final call number _____

3.4.11. Yiddish short stories.

    Base number _____

    Notation from Table 3-A _____

    Numbers to be added _____

    Final call number _____

3.4. Number Building from Tables

Table 3-B

3.4.12. A book of epic poetry.

Base number _____

Notation from Table 3-B _____

Numbers to be added _____

Final call number _____

3.4.13. A collection of adventure fiction.

Base number _____

Notation from Table 3-B _____

Numbers to be added _____

Final call number _____

3.4.14. A book of melodrama.

Base number _____

Notation from Table 3-B _____

Numbers to be added _____

Final call number _____

Table 3-C

3.4.15. A collection of literature in German and French about vampires.

Base number _____

Notation from Table 3-C _____

Numbers to be added _____

Final call number _____

3.4.16. A collection of humorous stories about sports heroes.

Base number _____

Notation from Table 3-C _____

76 Dewey Decimal Classification

Numbers to be added _____

Final call number _____

3.4.17. A collection of political speeches about education.

Base number _____

Notation from Table 3-C _____

Numbers to be added _____

Final call number _____

Table 4

3.4.18. A book about German syntax.

Base number _____

Notation from Table 4 _____

Numbers to be added _____

Final call number _____

3.4.19. A French reader for persons studying a second language.

Base number _____

Notation from Table 4 _____

Numbers to be added _____

Final call number _____

3.4.20. A dictionary of Hindi puns.

Base number _____

Notation from Table 4 _____

Numbers to be added _____

Final call number _____

3.4. Number Building from Tables

Table 5

3.4.21. A book on art of the Basque peoples.

Base number _____

Notation from Table 5 _____

Numbers to be added _____

Final call number _____

3.4.22. A book about Mongolian children.

Base number _____

Notation from Table 5 _____

Numbers to be added _____

Final call number _____

3.4.23. A book of Inuit astrology.

Base number _____

Notation from Table 5 _____

Numbers to be added _____

Final call number _____

Table 6

3.4.24. An encyclopedia written in Old Norse.

Base number _____

Notation from Table 6 _____

Numbers to be added _____

Final call number _____

3.4.25. A book on Vestinian grammar.

Base number _____

Notation from Table 6 _____

Numbers to be added _____

Final call number _____

78 Dewey Decimal Classification

3.4.26. Folk literature in the French language from Langue d'oc.

Base number _____

Notation from Table 6 _____

Numbers to be added _____

Final call number _____

Table 7

3.4.27. A book on art drawn by blind persons.

Base number _____

Notation from Table 7 _____

Numbers to be added _____

Final call number _____

3.4.28. A book on women firefighters.

Base number _____

Notation from Table 7 _____

Numbers to be added _____

Final call number _____

3.4.29. A book on the customs of meteorologists.

Base number _____

Notation from Table 7 _____

Numbers to be added _____

Final call number _____

3.5. Cutter Numbers

Charles Ammi Cutter devised a scheme to assign numbers that would keep books in order on a shelf in a designated fashion. Such numbers consist of one or two upper-case letters followed by one, two, or three numbers, and ending with one or two lower-case letters. The first letters would usually be the first letter or letters of the author's last name. The numbers come from the table that Cutter devised, and the final letter or letters designate the title of the work.

By assigning these contrived designations, works of fiction would be shelved together, by author, subdivided by title. By assigning Cutter numbers based on the last name of a biographee, all biographies of an individual would be shelved together. In this instance, the last letter or letters would be taken from the author's last name, thus putting the books about an individual together, in alphabetical order by author. If a work has a title main entry, the initial letters pertain to the title, and there are no ending letters.

The Cutter table is organized so that the letters following the author's initials are filed decimally, e.g., G35, G354, G42. The first letters of the alphabet have the earlier numbers, and the later letters have the later numbers. For example, Garden is coded G167; Gerry is G321; Gibbon is G352; Glover is G518; Gould is G729; Grand is G762; Grote is G915; and Guizot is G949. This Cuttering system is to be used with the Dewey Decimal system, as opposed to the LCC Cutter tables which would be used with the Library of Congress Classification system.

The following exercise was constructed using *C. A. Cutter's Three-Figure Author Table*, distributed by the H. R. Hunting Company. Answers from other editions, or those from the Cutter-Sanborn table, will be slightly different. In this edition, use one letter for words beginning with consonants (except S), two for words beginning with vowels and with S, and three for words beginning with SC. I, O, U, and X usually need only one digit. When two authors have the same last name, add a digit or use a preceding or succeeding number. As no titles have been associated with these names, you will not add the ending lower-case letters.

Cutter Table Exercises

3.5.1.   Jones, Rahula   _____

3.5.2.   Gary Ferguson   _____

3.5.3.   Sandy Colby   _____

3.5.4.   Carol Wines   _____

3.5.5.   Dana Watson   _____

3.5.6. Betty Lewis _____

3.5.7. Tessa Ryan Marchiafava _____

3.5.8. Sam Sharp _____

3.5.9. Christopher Sharp _____

3.5.10. Elisabeth Spanhoff _____

3.5.11. Lola Varughese _____

3.5.12. Lihong Zhu Dellenbarger _____

3.5.13. Judith Boyce _____

3.5.14. Dana Robertson _____

3.5.15. Jennifer Seneca _____

3.5.16. Charles Patterson _____

3.5.17. Terre Buckelew _____

3.5.18. Elizabeth Sewell   _____

3.5.19. Fannie Easterly   _____

3.5.20. Katharine Martin   _____

3.5.21. Sheila Intner   _____

3.5.22. Arthur Upfield   _____

3.5.23. Tony O'Connor   _____

3.5.24. Bruce Allen   _____

3.5.25. Louise Young   _____

3.5.26. Southerby Smith   _____

3.5.27. Allen Zelig   _____

3.5.28. George Kontos   _____

3.5.29. Robert Ewing   _____

3.5.30. Marcia Lea   _____

3.5.31. Anneliese Meck   _____

3.5.32. Betty Jo Finley   _____

4.
LIBRARY OF CONGRESS CLASSIFICATION

Introduction

Although the classification scheme used currently in the Library of Congress was designed for that institution only, it has been adopted by a great number of libraries in the United States and Canada and throughout the world. It was not intended to be a perfect system when it was originally created, and was expected to be expanded as needed. It has indeed been revised and expanded over the years since its creation in 1898, and is still evolving to fit the needs of the Library of Congress and of other libraries that use it.

The scheme is divided into twenty-one basic areas of knowledge, subdivided into smaller units, and further subdivided into topic, form, place, and time. It is a system that uses letters (single, double, or triple) and numerals (1–9999) in numerical, not decimal, order. As the system has expanded, however, certain areas that have no breaks (unused numbers) have had decimal segments added to make the system more specific.

Cutter numbers, originally devised by Charles Ammi Cutter, are added to the classification number to ensure that books with the same number are shelved in alphabetical order. The practice is used with both the Dewey Decimal and the Library of Congress systems. Over the years library jargon has referred to the assigning of these numbers as "Cuttering."

Cutter numbers for authors are assigned from a table (see p. 86) and are a combination of an upper-case letter followed by (usually) two Arabic numerals. A particular author does not have a single Cutter used in all cases; the Cutter differs so as to create alphabetical order within each class.

Cutter numbers may be assigned from the main entry, or they can be specified within the class number to bring out a second aspect of the subject matter—form, period, place, or subtopic. The first Cutter in each LCC number is preceded by a period. The second Cutter is appended to the first. The publication date of the work is always added to the end of the Cutter number. If two editions of the work are issued within the same year, the first to be received at the library is designated with a lower-case *a* (*1997a*), and the second to be received is designated with a *b* (*1997b*).

Some classes have auxiliary tables used for assigning specific numbers within a range of numbers from the main schedule. Tables may be of general or limited application, and may refer to an entire class or to a subclass only. Some examples of general-application tables are the geographic tables based on Cutter numbers, biography tables, and translation tables.

Limited-application tables may take the form of numerical tables, Cutter tables, or a combination of the two. One example is the form table in Class K.

Individual schedules of the LC classification system were developed separately by different working groups and are therefore less uniform than other classification systems, such as Dewey. There are some unifying characteristics common to all schedules, such as introductory notes, an outline of the schedule and subclasses, the schedule itself, accompanying tables, and an index to the individual schedule (there is no overall index to the entire scheme).

The individual schedules use the same basic order of numbers, although the actual numbers vary somewhat between classes. Schedules begin with periodicals, and are followed by yearbooks, societies, congresses, collected works, dictionaries and encyclopedias, terminology, directories, history, biography, theory, and so on. General works are usually given a single upper-case letter, followed by digits in numerical order. Subclasses use double upper-case letters, and are followed by digits in the same basic order. For example: in class H (Social Sciences), an English-language dictionary of sociology might be assigned the number H41; a dictionary dealing with statistics HA17, and a dictionary of public finance might be placed in HJ121. As each schedule and subclass is different, catalogers must use care in assigning numbers.

Library of Congress Classifications

A	General works
B-BJ	Philosophy. Psychology
BL-BX	Religion
C	Auxiliary Sciences of History
D	History: General and Old World (Eastern Hemisphere)
E-F	History: America (Western Hemisphere)
G	Geography. Anthropology. Recreation
H	Social Sciences
J	Political Science
K	Law (General)
KD-KKC	Law of other continents and countries
KF	Law of the United States
L	Education
M	Music. Books on Music
N	Fine Arts
P-PA	General Philology and Linguistics. Classical Languages and Literatures
PB-PH	Modern European Languages
PG	Russian Literature
PJ-PM	Languages and Literatures of Asia, Africa, Oceania. American Indian Languages. Artificial Languages
PM Supp.	Index to Languages and Dialects
PN,PR,PS,PZ	General Literature. English and American Literature. Fiction in English. Juvenile Belles Lettres
PQ	French, Italian, Spanish, and Portuguese Literatures
PT	German, Dutch, and Scandinavian Literatures
Q	Science
R	Medicine
S	Agriculture
T	Technology
U	Military Science
V	Naval Science
Z	Bibliography. Library Science

Cutter Table

1) After initial vowels

for the second letter:	b	d	l–m	n	p	r	s–t	u–y
use number:	2	3	4	5	6	7	8	9

2) After initial letter S

for the second letter:	a	ch	e	h–i	m–p	t	u	w–z
use number:	2	3	4	5	6	7	8	9

3) After initial letters Qu

for the second letter:	a	e	i	o	r	t	y
use number:	3	4	5	6	7	8	9

for initial letters Qa–Qt, use: 2–29

4) After other initial consonants

for the second letter:	a	e	i	o	r	u	y
use number:	3	4	5	6	7	8	9

5) For expansion

for the letter:	a–d	e–h	i–l	m–o	p–s	t–v	w–z
use number:	3	4	5	6	7	8	9

4.1. LCC Author Cutter Exercises

Give the author Cutters for the following names. Use the Cutter table on page 86.

4.1.1. Chris Stringer   _____

4.1.2. Jacquelin Gorman   _____

4.1.3. Joel Millman   _____

4.1.4. Pauline Maier   _____

4.1.5. Roger Lane   _____

4.1.6. John R. Horner   _____

4.1.7. Aaron Latham   _____

4.1.8. Elaine DePrince   _____

4.1.9. Sylvia Morris   _____

4.1.10. Philip Van Munching   _____

4.1.11. Wallis Wilde-Menozzi   _____

4.1.12. Robert Sharp   _____

4.1.13. Aleksandr Fursenko   _____

4.1.14. Wesley Smith   _____

4.1.15. Nicols Fox   _____

4.1.16. Colleen Dewhurst   _____

4.1.17. William Ayers   _____

4.1.18. Laurence Leamer   _____

4.1.19. Isabella Rossellini   _____

4.1.20. Sandra Steingraber   _____

88   Library of Congress Classification

4.1.21. David Freedman _____

4.1.22. Stephen Hall _____

4.1.23. Jim Cullen _____

4.1.24. Julia Stewart _____

4.1.25. Shane Anderson _____

4.1.26. Bert Dievert _____

4.1.27. Mark Patton _____

4.1.28. J. Michael Hayes _____

4.1.29. Stephen Lambert _____

4.1.30. Jean Reed _____

4.1.31. Roger McIntire _____

4.1.32. Thomas Watters _____

4.1.33. Russell Bourne _____

4.1.34. Tim Snyder _____

4.1.35. Judy Brown _____

4.2. LCC Outline Exercises

Go to the outline of schedules on page 85. Find the volume of the Library of Congress classification schedule in which you would find each of the following subjects. Put the general class letters in the blank.

4.2.1.   Juvenile fiction _____

4.2.2.   African literature _____

4.2.3.   Military science _____

4.2.4.   Library science _____

4.2.5. Medicine   _____

4.2.6. German literature _____

4.2.7. United States law _____

4.2.8. Religion   _____

4.2.9. Political science _____

4.2.10. Fine arts   _____

4.2.11. Naval science   _____

4.2.12. Education   _____

4.2.13. Social sciences _____

4.2.14. American history _____

4.2.15. Agriculture   _____

4.3. LCC Exercises, Set 1

Use the given subject heading to determine the probable subject matter of the items shown below. Determine the correct LCC and write it on the line.

4.3.1. Author: Sanson, Jacques.
Title: A history of the guillotine. (1997)
LCSH: Guillotines.

LCC: _____

4.3.2. Author: Riteway, Jill.
Title: Quick pasta dishes for the working woman. (1995)
LCSH: Cookery (Pasta)

LCC: _____

4.3.3. Author: Stuck, William.
Title: Country teas. (1997)
LCSH: Afternoon teas--United States.

Library of Congress Classification

LCC: _____

4.3.4. Author: Leon, Marvin W.
Title: He's at it again: the reawakening of Hitler. (1996)
LCSH: Neo-Nazism.

LCC: _____

4.3.5. Author: Eddington, Roger B.
Title: Warriors in the rising sun. (1994)
LCSH: Military policy--Japan.

LCC: _____

4.3.6. Author: Lewis, Marvin.
Title: Trail fever: Clinton's efforts to down Bush. (1991)
LCSH: Presidents--United States--Election--1992.

LCC: _____

4.3.7. Author: Kovel, Bento Shriver.
Title: Justice overturned. (1996)
LCSH: Criminal justice, Administration of--United States.

LCC: _____

4.3.8. Author: Terry, Jonathan.
Title: The next war. (1997)
LCSH: Transnational crime.

LCC: _____

4.3.9. Author: Austin, William B.
Title: I ache all over: why we have to age. (1996)
LCSH: Aging--Physiological aspects.

LCC: _____

4.3.10. Author: Berry, Deborah.
Title: An overview of the ancient Egyptians. (1997)
LCSH: Egypt--Civilization--To 332 B.C.

LCC: _____

4.3.11. Author: McCarthy, Todd.
Title: Howard Hawks. (1997)
LCSH: Motion picture producers and directors--Biography.

LCC: _____

4.3. LCC Exercises, Set 1 91

4.3.12. Author: Hirschman, Dave.
Title: Hijacked. (1996)
LCSH: Hijacking of aircraft--United States.

LCC: _____

4.3.13. Author: Warren, Wally.
Title: Who's next? (1997)
LCSH: Downsizing of organizations.

LCC: _____

4.3.14. Author: Smith, Richard T.
Title: The Chief: a biography of Marcus Lucius. (1996)
LCSH: Newspaper editors--United States--Biography.

LCC: _____

4.3.15. Author: Strege, John.
Title: Tiger. (1997)
LCSH: Golfers--United States--Biography.

LCC: _____

4.3.16. Author: Spoto, Donald.
Title: Notorious: the life of Ingrid Bergman. (1997)
LCSH: Motion picture actors and actresses--Biography.

LCC: _____

4.3.17. Author: Mandrake, Robert L.
Title: Here they come at last!: how fighter pilots are trained. (1994)
LCSH: Fighter pilots--Training of--Florida--Jacksonville.

LCC: _____

4.3.18. Author: Warren, Earl.
Title: Chief justice: my autobiography. (1989)
LCSH: Judges--United States--Biography.

LCC: _____

4.3.19. Author: Garcia Lorca, Jesus Maria.
Title: News of a kidnapping: Juan Jimenez never returned. (1996)
LCSH: Kidnapping--Colombia.

LCC: _____

92 Library of Congress Classification

4.3.20. Author: Toland, John.
Title: Captured by history. (1997)
LCSH: Historians--United States--Biography.

LCC: _____

4.4. LCC Exercises, Set 2

Use the most current edition of the appropriate Library of Congress classification schedules to find the correct LC number and write it on the line. You do not have information on authors or publication dates, so exclude these elements of the classification number.

4.4.1. A book about caring for people with Alzheimer's. _____

4.4.2. A book about eating disorders. _____

4.4.3. A book of Gary Larson cartoons. _____

4.4.4. A book about making valances. _____

4.4.5. A book about texture painting in bedrooms. _____

4.4.6. A directory of retirement communities in the United States. _____

4.4.7. A dictionary of jargon for developmentally disabled children. _____

4.4.8. A general work on old age pensions in the United States. _____

4.4.9. Monologues for recitation. _____

4.4.10. Modern interpretation of Sophocles. _____

4.4.11. A book about teaching report writing. _____

4.4.12. Assistance to handicapped women. _____

4.4.13. A book about improving your memory. _____

4.4.14. A German book about dream interpretation. _____

4.4.15. A modern book on ancient Greek religion. _____

4.4.16. Different ways to wrap gifts. _____

4.4. LCC Exercises, Set 2

4.4.17. A list of baby names from the Bible. _____

4.4.18. A book about writing plays in English. _____

4.4.19. A book on osteoarthritis. _____

4.4.20. A book about making Italian desserts. _____

4.4.21. A book about sex in man-woman relationships. _____

4.4.22. A book about the history of motion pictures in Hollywood. _____

4.4.23. A book on human evolution, or the origin of man. _____

4.4.24. A general work on schools for guide dogs. _____

4.4.25. A book on the economic and social aspects of immigration. _____

4.4.26. A book about the Declaration of Independence. _____

4.4.27. A book about the history of murder in America. _____

4.4.28. A book on dinosaurs. _____

4.4.29. A book about love in American old age. _____

4.4.30. A book about the causes of AIDS. _____

4.4.31. A book about the beer industry in the United States. _____

4.4.32. A book about the Roman Catholic Church in America. _____

4.4.33. A biography of Americans living in Parma, Italy. _____

4.4.34. A book about travel in Iran after Khomeini. _____

4.4.35. A book about the Cuban missile crisis of 1962. _____

4.4.36. A book about the ethics of assisted suicide. _____

4.4.37. A book about foodborne diseases. _____

4.4.38. A biography of Colleen Dewhurst. _____

4.4.39. A book about juvenile delinquency in Chicago.

4.4.40. A history of country music in Nashville.

4.4.41. A biography of Isabella Rossellini.

4.4.42. A book about environmental toxicology.

4.4.43. A book about computer crime in the USA.

4.4.44. A book about immunotherapy.

4.4.45. A book of criticism and interpretation of Bruce Springsteen.

4.4.46. A dictionary of French surnames.

4.4.47. A miscellanea of Lincoln cent information.

4.4.48. A directory of film and video producers.

4.4.49. Writing personal statements for college applications.

4.4.50. An outline of attorney and client communication.

4.4.51. A book on vocational guidance for sociologists.

4.4.52. A book on writing resumes.

4.4.53. A book on parental relations with adolescents.

4.4.54. A juvenile book about the planets.

4.4.55. A history of inventions in America.

4.4.56. A book on building shelving and storage.

4.4.57. A book on vegetarian cookery.

4.4.58. A book on design and construction of tables.

4.4.59. A book on low-fat diets.

BIBLIOGRAPHY

> Ninety-nine percent of being thought a genius consists
> of knowing who to ask for information!
>
> —Trey Lewis, Director
> Red River Parish Library

General Materials

ALA Glossary of Library and Information Science. Chicago: American Library Association, 1982.

Chan, Lois Mai. *Cataloging and Classification: An Introduction.* 2d ed. New York: McGraw-Hill, 1994.

Chan, Lois Mai, et al. *Dewey Decimal Classification: A Practical Guide.* 2d ed. rev. for *DDC21.* Albany, NY: OCLC/Forest Press, 1996.

Downing, Mildred Harlow, and David H. Downing. *Introduction to Cataloging and Classification.* 6th ed., rev. and greatly enlarged in accordance with *AACR2R88* and *DDC20.* Jefferson, NC: McFarland, 1992.

Intner, Sheila S., and Jean Weihs. *Standard Cataloging for School and Public Libraries.* 2d ed. Englewood, CO: Libraries Unlimited, 1996.

Saye, Jerry D., and Desretta V. McAllister-Harper. *Manheimer's Cataloging and Classification: A Workbook.* 3d ed., rev. and expanded. New York: Marcel Dekker, 1991.

Soper, Mary Ellen, et al. *Librarians' Thesaurus: A Concise Guide to Library and Information Terms.* Chicago: American Library Association, 1990.

Winkle, Lois, ed. *Subject Headings for Children: A List of Subject Headings Used by the Library of Congress with Dewey Numbers Added.* 2 vols. Albany, NY: OCLC/Forest Press, 1994.

Wynar, Bohdan S. *Introduction to Cataloging and Classification*. 8th ed., edited by Arlene G. Taylor. Englewood, CO: Libraries Unlimited, 1992.

Special Materials

Anglo-American Cataloguing Rules. 2d ed., 1988 revision. Prepared under the direction of the Joint Steering Committee for Revision of AACR, a committee of the American Library Association, the Australian Committee on Cataloguing, the British Library, the Canadian Committee on Cataloguing, the Library Association, the Library of Congress. Edited by Michael Gorman and Paul W. Winkler. Chicago: American Library Association, 1988.

DDC21. Joan Mitchell, ed. 4 vols. Albany, NY: OCLC/Forest Press, 1996.

Library of Congress. Cataloging Policy and Support Office. *Free-Floating Subdivisions: An Alphabetical Index*. 9th ed. Washington, DC: Library of Congress, 1997.

Library of Congress. Cataloging Policy and Support Office. *Library of Congress Subject Headings*. 20th ed. Washington, DC: Library of Congress, 1997.

Library of Congress. Cataloging Policy and Support Office. *Subject Cataloging Manual: Subject Headings*. 5th ed. Washington, DC: Library of Congress, 1996.

Library of Congress. Subject Cataloging Division. *Classification*. Washington, DC: Library of Congress, 1901– .

Sears List of Subject Headings. 16th ed., edited by Joseph Miller. New York: H.W. Wilson, 1997.

Periodicals and Serials

Cataloging & Classification Quarterly. Binghamton, NY: Haworth Press, 1980– . Quarterly.

Cataloging Service Bulletin. Washington, DC: Library of Congress, 1978– . Quarterly.

Library Resources & Technical Services. Chicago: American Library Association, 1982– . Quarterly.

Technical Services Quarterly. Binghamton, NY: Haworth Press, 1983– . Quarterly.

Technicalities. Kansas City, MO: Media Services Publications, 1981– . Monthly.

ANSWER KEY

1.1. *LCSH* Subject Heading Exercise Answers

These are suggested answers. You may have others that also fit the description given in the exercise.

1.1.1.
- A. Long, Huey Pierce, 1893–1935.
- B. Louisiana--Politics and government.
- C. Governors--Louisiana--Biography.

1.1.2.
- A. Louisiana. Dept. of Education--History.
- B. Education and state--Louisiana.
- C. Louisiana--Officials and employees.
- D. Education--Louisiana--History.

1.1.3.
- A. Tunica Indians--Social life and customs.
- B. Biloxi Indians--Social life and customs.
- C. Indians of North America--Southern States--Social life and customs.

1.1.4.
- A. United States--History--Civil War, 1861-1865--Participation, Afro-American.
- B. Afro-American soldiers--United States--History--Civil War, 1861-1865.
- C. United States. Army--Afro-American troops.
- D. United States--History, Military.

1.1.5.
- A. New Orleans (La.)--Social life and customs.
- B. Plantations--Louisiana--New Orleans.
- C. Plantation life--Louisiana--New Orleans.
- D. Historic buildings--Louisiana--New Orleans.

1.1.6.
- A. Oil and gas leases--Mexico, Gulf of.
- B. Petroleum law and legislation--Mexico, Gulf of.
- C. Marine mineral resources--Mexico, Gulf of--Prospecting.
- D. Petroleum industry and trade--Mexico, Gulf of.
- E. Offshore oil industry--Mexico, Gulf of.
- F. Petroleum in submerged lands--Mexico, Gulf of.

1.1.7.
- A. Library architecture--Louisiana.
- B. Architecture--Awards--Louisiana.
- C. Libraries--Louisiana--Designs and plans.
- D. Library decoration.

Answer Key

1.1.8. A. Hibbert family.
        B. New Orleans (La.)--Genealogy.
        C. New Orleans (La.)--Biography.

1.1.9. A. Salt domes.
        B. Hazardous waste sites--Law and legislation.
        C. Waste disposal in the ground--Law and legislation.

1.1.10. A. Roads--Environmental aspects--Georgia--Cobb County.
        B. Highway planning--Georgia--Cobb County.
        C. Highway planning--Citizen participation.

1.1.11. A. Flood damage prevention--Pennsylvania--Johnstown.
        B. Drainage--Pennsylvania--Johnstown.
        C. Flood forecasting--Pennsylvania--Johnstown.

1.1.12. A. School enrollment--Louisiana--Florida Parishes--History.
        B. Florida Parishes (La.)--History--Eighteenth century.
        C. Education--Louisiana--Florida Parishes--History--Eighteenth century.

1.1.13. A. Arpadhon (La.)--History.
        B. Arpadhon (La.)--Biography.
        C. Hungarian Americans--Louisiana--Arpadhon.

1.1.14. A. Sarajevo (Bosnia and Hercegovina)--Politics and government.
        B. Sarajevo (Bosnia and Hercegovina)--History--Siege, 1992-
        C. Bosnians--Personal narratives.

1.1.15. A. Operation Desert Shield, 1990-1991.
        B. United States. Army--Foreign service--Iran.
        C. Persian Gulf War, 1991.

1.1.16. A. Printing-press--Germany--History--Eighteenth century.
        B. Printing--Germany--History--Eighteenth century.
        C. Printing industry--Germany--History--Eighteenth century.

1.1.17. A. AIDS (Disease)--Patients--Case studies.
        B. Autoimmune diseases--Hospice care.
        C. AIDS (Disease)--Complications--Case studies.

1.1.18. A. Euthanasia.
        B. Death--Moral and ethical aspects.
        C. Death--Religious aspects.

1.1.19. A. Great Wall of China (China)--History.
        B. China--History--Ch'in dynasty, 221-207 B.C.
        C. Fortifications--China.

1.1.20. A. Nixon, Richard M. (Richard Milhous), 1913-
        B. Presidents--United States--Biography.
        C. Governors--California--Biography.

1.1. LCSH Subject Heading Exercise Answers

1.1.21. A. Plantations--Virginia--Richmond Region.
        B. Plantation life--Virginia--Richmond Region.
        C. Historic buildings--Virginia--Richmond Region.

1.1.22. A. Missoula (Mont.). Office of the Mayor.
        B. Missoula (Mont.)--Politics and government.
        C. Local government--Montana--Missoula.

1.1.23. A. Cherokee Indians--Social life and customs.
        B. Cherokee Indians--Marriage customs and rites.
        C. Cherokee women--Social life and customs.

1.1.24. A. Alabama--History--Civil War, 1861-1865.
        B. Veterans--Alabama--Records.
        C. Alabama--Genealogy.

1.1.25. A. Pipelines--Alaska--Design and construction.
        B. Pipelines--Alaska--Maintenance.
        C. Trans-Alaska Pipeline--History.

1.1.26. A. Louisiana irises--Encyclopedias.
        B. Iris (Plant)--Encyclopedias.
        C. Louisiana irises--Varieties.

1.1.27. A. Junk bonds--Law and legislation.
        B. Bonds--Ratings--Law and legislation.
        C. Stock exchanges--Law and legislation.

1.1.28. A. Whitfield family.
        B. Shawnee (Kans.)--Biography.
        C. Shawnee (Kans.)--Genealogy.

1.1.29. A. Hurricane Andrew, 1992.
        B. Hurricanes--Florida.
        C. Hurricanes--Louisiana.

1.1.30. A. Freight and freightage--New York--History--19th century.
        B. Waterways--New York--History--19th century.
        C. Erie Canal (N.Y.)--History--19th century.

1.1.31. A. Isleto Indians--New Mexico--History.
        B. New Mexico--Ethnic relations.
        C. Frontier and pioneer life--New Mexico.

1.1.32. A. Bridges--Missouri--Saint Louis--Planning.
        B. Highway planning--Missouri--Saint Louis--Citizen participation.
        C. Bridges--Mississippi River--Planning.

1.1.33. A. All terrain vehicles--Maintenance and repair.
        B. Dune buggies--Maintenance and repair.
        C. Snowmobiles--Maintenance and repair.

1.1.34. A. Mount Everest Expedition, 1922.
         B. Mount Everest Expedition, 1924.
         C. Mount Everest Expedition, 1938.
         D. Everest, Mount (China and Nepal)--Description and travel.
         E. Mountaineering--Everest, Mount (China and Nepal)

1.1.35. A. Panizzi, Anthony.
         B. Librarians--Biography.
         C. British Museum--History.

1.1.36. A. Domes--Design and construction.
         B. Architecture--Details.
         C. Finials--Design and construction.

1.2. *LCSH* Subject Heading Terminology Exercise Answers

1.2.1. Antibiotics in animal nutrition.
Plants, Effect of antibiotics on.

1.2.2. Chin--Surgery.
Surgery, Plastic.

1.2.3. Caucasian race.
Latin peoples.
Greeks.

1.2.4. Ragwort, Tansy.
Ragwort groundsel.
Senscio jacobaea.

1.2.5. --Automation.
--Electric equipment.
--Heating and ventilation.
--Production standards.
--Vocational guidance.

1.2.6. --Agents.
--Catastrophic.
--Long-term care.
--Rates and tables.
--Selling.

1.2.7. Yes.

1.2.8. No.

1.2.9. No.

1.2.10. Berget family.
Birge family.
Borg family.
Van den Bergh family.

1.2.11. Names of berries, e.g., **Strawberries**.

1.2.12. No.

1.2.13. Yes, --**Religious aspects**.

1.2.14. 111.

1.2.15. Backbone.

1.2.16. (BT) **Natural products** ; (NT) **Coal-tar** and **Wood tar**.

1.2.17. Yes, **Books, Expurgated**.

1.2.18. Yes, **Black power**.

1.2.19. **Occupational diseases** and **Toxicology**.

1.2.20. Occupational diseases.

1.2.21. Yes, (BT) **Insignia** and (NT) **Decorations of honor**.

1.2.22. Not under the main heading **Orders of knighthood and chivalry--Insignia**, but there is a definitive scope note under the main heading **Insignia**.

1.2.23. The broader term is **Streets--Pennsylvania**, telling you that Franklin Court must be a street.

1.2.24. Black hawk eagle.

1.2.25. **Equus** and **Zebras**.

1.3. *LCSH* Geographic Subdivisions Exercise Answers

1.3.1. Design, Industrial--Law and legislation--Missouri--Kansas City.

1.3.2. Art, Tibetan--France--Paris.
Drawing, Tibetan--France--Paris.

1.3.3. Carpentry--Vocational guidance--Wisconsin--Milwaukee.

1.3.4. Wildlife conservation--Law and legislation--Georgia.
Game-laws--Georgia.

1.3.5. Gamgee family. [and] Norman (Okla.)--Genealogy.

1.3.6. Motion pictures--India--Bombay--Editing--History.

1.3.7. Humor in education--History.
Schools--Utah--Humor.

1.3.8. Molds (Cookware)--Louisiana--Design.

102 Answer Key

1.3.9. Industries--Defense measures--Nebraska.

1.3.10. Shanholtzer family. [and] New Jersey--Genealogy.

1.3.11. Anthropology--China--Video tape catalogs.

1.3.12. Piano--Recitals--Germany--Hamburg.

1.3.13. Deer hunting--Colorado.

1.3.14. Presidents--South Africa--Election.

1.3.15. Forests and forestry--Contests--Canada--Yukon.
Logrolling (Aquatic sports)--Canada--Yukon.

1.3.16. Pipelines--Alaska--Design and construction.

1.3.17. Cookery (Beans)
Low-fat foods--Texas--Laredo.

1.3.18. Belgian draft horse--Kentucky--Breeding.

1.3.19. Explosives--Transportation--Missouri--Kansas City.

1.3.20. Juvenile delinquents--Rehabilitation--New York (State)--New York.

1.3.21. Pro-life movement--New Jersey--New Brunswick.

1.3.22. Animal welfare--Nebraska--Omaha.

1.3.23. Great spotted woodpeckers--Nests--Idaho--Boise.

1.3.24. Navy-yards and naval stations--Europe--Directories.

1.3.25. Vienna porcelain--Forgeries--France.

1.3.26. Color separation--Hawaii--Oahu--Directories.

1.3.27. Invertebrates, Fossil--China--Textbooks.

1.3.28. Phlebobranchia--Chile--Identification.

1.3.29. Quick-cooking rice--Propagation--Louisiana--Handbooks, manuals, etc.

1.3.30. Angels--Cult--California--Los Angeles--History.

1.3.31. Jukun language--Grammar--Nigeria.

1.3.32. Manila clam--Massachusetts--Cape Cod--Fisheries.

1.3.33. Umbrella industry--Washington (State)--Seattle.

1.4. Pattern Headings Exercise Answers

1.4.1. Basic subject   Cajun French dialect
Pattern heading to be used   English language
Full subject heading   Cajun French dialect--History.

1.4. Pattern Headings Exercise Answers

1.4.2.	Basic subject	Frost resistant concrete
	Pattern heading to be used	Concrete
	Full subject heading	Frost resistant concrete--Testing.
1.4.3.	Basic subject	Lambs
	Pattern heading to be used	Cattle
	Full subject heading	Lambs--Pedigrees--Handbooks, manuals, etc.
1.4.4.	Basic subject	Petroleum industry and trade
	Pattern heading to be used	Construction industry
	Full subject heading	Petroleum industry and trade--Corrupt practices--Texas.
1.4.5.	Basic subject	Myasthenia gravis
	Pattern heading to be used	Cancer
	Full subject heading	Myasthenia gravis--Genetic aspects.
1.4.6.	Basic subject	Byron, George Gordon Byron, Baron
	Pattern heading to be used	Shakespeare, William, 1564-1616
	Full subject heading	Byron, George Gordon Byron, Baron--Homes and haunts--Italy--Venice.
1.4.7.	Basic subject	Gnus
	Pattern heading to be used	Fishes
	Full subject heading	Gnus--Migration.
1.4.8.	Basic subject	Baptists--Clergy
	Pattern heading to be used	Catholic Church
	Full subject heading	Baptists--Clergy--Health and hygiene--California--Los Angeles.
1.4.9.	Basic subject	Hong Kong
	Pattern heading to be used	Great Britain--Colonies
	Full subject heading	Hong Kong--Defenses.
1.4.10.	Basic subject	Harp
	Pattern heading to be used	Piano
	Full subject heading	Harp--Catalogs and collections.
1.4.11.	Basic subject	Wheat
	Pattern heading to be used	Corn
	Full subject heading	Wheat--Diseases and pests--Louisiana--Rapides Parish--Congresses.

Answer Key

1.4.12. Basic subject — France--Colonies
Pattern heading to be used — Great Britain--Colonies
Full subject heading — France--Colonies--Boundaries.

1.4.13. Basic subject — Franciscans
Pattern heading to be used — Jesuits
Full subject heading — Franciscans--Customs and practices.

1.4.14. Basic subject — Royal Canadian Air Force
Pattern heading to be used — United States. Air Force
Full subject heading — Royal Canadian Air Force --Ground support.

1.4.15. Basic subject — Spanish-American War, 1898
Pattern heading to be used — United States--History--Civil War, 1861-1865.
Full subject heading — Spanish-American War, 1898-- Cavalry operations.

1.4.16. Basic subject — Medical personnel--Malpractice
Pattern heading to be used — Labor laws and legislation
Full subject heading — Medical personnel--Malpractice --Compliance costs.

1.4.17. Basic subject — Quartz
Pattern heading to be used — Copper
Full subject heading — Quartz--Oxidation--Washington (State)--Seattle.

1.4.18. Basic subject — Colon
Pattern heading to be used — Heart
Full subject heading — Colon--Diseases --Psychosomatic aspects.

1.4.19. Basic subject — Monghol language
Pattern heading to be used — English language
Full subject heading — Monghol language--Capitalization.

1.4.20. Basic subject — Tibetan literature
Pattern heading to be used — English literature
Full subject heading — Tibetan literature --American influences.

1.4.21.	Basic subject	Welty, Eudora
	Pattern heading to be used	Shakespeare, William, 1564-1616
	Full subject heading	Welty, Eudora--Language --Punctuation.
1.4.22.	Basic subject	Pavements, Asphalt
	Pattern heading to be used	Concrete
	Full subject heading	Pavements, Asphalt--Moisture --Measurement.
1.4.23.	Basic subject	Hummer (All terrain vehicle)
	Pattern heading to be used	Automobiles
	Full subject heading	Hummer (All terrain vehicle)--Bodies --Alignment.

1.5. Inverted Heading versus Subdivision or Phrase Heading Exercise Answers

1.5.1.	X	American newspapers.
1.5.2.	X	Folklore--Ukraine.
1.5.3.	X	Ballads, English.
1.5.4.	X	French literature.
1.5.5.	X	Presidents--France.
1.5.6.	X	German newspapers.
1.5.7.	X	Mongolian periodicals.
1.5.8.	X	Bridge players.
1.5.9.	X	Cookery, German.
1.5.10.	X	Divergent thinking.
1.5.11.	X	Divorce mediation.
1.5.12.	X	Families, Black.
1.5.13.	X	Frost hazard.
1.5.14.	X	Guatemalan poetry.
1.5.15.	X	Haggadot, Kibbutz.
1.5.16.	X	Iron sculpture, Buddhist.
1.5.17.	X	John, the Baptist, Saint.
1.5.18.	X	Navies, Cost of.
1.5.19.	X	Protective coatings.
1.5.20.	X	Proteins--Denaturation.

106 Answer Key

1.5.21.	X	Railroads--Train dispatching.
1.5.22.	X	Barite rosettes.
1.5.23.	X	Artificial respiration.
1.5.24.	X	Restorations, Political.

1.6. Annotated Card Program Exercise Answers

1.6.1. Treasure hunts.

1.6.2. Pets.

1.6.3. Reproduction.
Childbirth.

1.6.4. Bridge whist.
Contract bridge.

1.6.5. --Spelling.
--Textbooks for foreign speakers.

1.6.6. --Orthography and spelling.

1.6.7. Yes.

1.6.8. Card tricks.
Magic.

1.6.9. Stories in rhyme.

1.6.10. Literary recreations.

1.6.11. No—they are already juvenile, intended for a juvenile audience.

1.6.12. AC: Mystery and detective stories.
Adult: Detective and mystery stories.

1.6.13. Altai (Turkish people)--Folklore.

1.6.14. Animation (Cinematography)

1.6.15. Christianity--History.

1.6.16. Juvenile: Boxing--Fiction.
Adult: Boxing stories.

1.6.17. Additional entries to be made.

1.7. *LCSH* Scope Note Exercise Answers

1.7.1. For works on persons hired as guides for fishers.

1.7.2. Yes, *See also* **Married women--Legal status, laws, etc.**

1.7.3. No.

1.7.4. An explanatory note giving the meaning of the heading.

1.7.5. Yes.

1.7.6. Yes.

1.7.7. The first is for comprehensive works on the Olympics, and the second is for works on a specific event.

1.7.8. Yes.

1.7.9. No.

1.8. *Subject Cataloging Manual* and *Free-Floating Subdivisions* Exercise Answers

1.8.1. These subdivisions may be form subdivisions. This is an innovation first appearing in the 9th edition.

1.8.2. Classes of persons; Ethnic groups; Corporate bodies; Individual persons; Individual literary authors.

1.8.3. Yes.

1.8.4. No.

1.8.5. Yes.

1.8.6. The category given for this subdivision is **Military services**. It cannot therefore be used for any other category.

1.8.7. Yes. One example is **Handicapped children--Home care**. It is a free-floating subdivision under Classes of Persons, and is also listed in *LCSH*.

1.8.8. Yes.

1.8.9. --**Statistics**, --**Statistics, Medical**, and --**Statistics, Vital**.

1.8.10. They are given a diamond shape on the left, beside the hyphen.

1.8.11. In the Index.

1.8.12. No. You must use --**Language--Dialects**.

1.8.13. Yes.

1.8.14. No.

1.8.15. Yes. [See Section H 1110 for examples.]

1.8.16. The first is about the use of --**Delta** and the second is about the use of --**Estuary**.

1.8.17. Yes.

1.8.18. H 1285, 3.a. (General works on individual battles) and b. (Special topics).

1.8.19. Three. Major civilizations; Major religious groups; and Ethnic groups, religious sects, ancient peoples, etc.

1.8.20. By free-floating period subdivisions under the subdivision --**Civilization**; by other period subdivisions; by civilizations of narrow time periods; or by special civilizations of particular places.

1.8.21. In August 1996.

1.8.22. They must be 1) formally convened; 2) directed toward a common goal; 3) capable of being reconvened; 4) have formal names, locations, dates, and durations that can be determined in advance of the event.

1.8.23. No.

1.8.24. Grade 9, age 15.

1.8.25. H 1845.

1.8.26. Ten.

1.8.27. At least 50%.

1.8.28. No.

1.8.29. Only when the work is *about* the program; if it is the software itself, do not assign the name of the program as a subject heading.

1.8.30. Eleven. They include: Continuing education, Early childhood, Elementary, Graduate, Higher, Internship, Middle school, Preschool, Primary, Residency, Secondary.

1.8.31. In the appendix in volume 4.

1.8.32. No.

1.8.33. In Appendix D, Punctuation.

1.8.34. Yes.

1.8.35. No.

1.9. *LCSH* History Subdivisions Exercise Answers

1.9.1. ≠a Germany ≠x History ≠y To 843.
≠a Teutoburger Wald, Battle of, 9 A.D.

1.9.2. ≠a China ≠x History ≠y Ch'in dynasty, 221-207 B.C. ≠x Humor.

1.9. *LCSH* History Subdivisions Exercise Answers

1.9.3. ≠a United States ≠x History ≠y Colonial period, ca. 1600-1775.

1.9.4. ≠a Canada ≠x History ≠y To 1763 (New France)
≠a Champlain, Lake, Battle of, 1609.

1.9.5. ≠a France ≠x History ≠y To 987.
≠a Carolingians ≠x History.

1.9.6. ≠a Greece ≠x History ≠y To 146 B.C.
≠a Issus, Battle of, 333 B.C.

1.9.7. ≠a Germany ≠x History ≠y Otto IV, 1208-1214.

1.9.8. ≠a France ≠x History ≠y Capetians, 987-1328.
≠a Latin Empire, 1204-1261.

1.9.9. ≠a China ≠x History ≠y 220-589.

1.9.10. ≠a Canada ≠x History ≠y 19th century ≠x Juvenile literature.

1.9.11. ≠a Greece ≠x History ≠y Athenian supremacy, 479-431 B.C.

1.9.12. ≠a United States ≠x History ≠y King William's War, 1689-1697.
≠x Biography.

1.9.13. ≠a Germany ≠x History ≠y Revolution, 1848-1849 ≠x Refugees.

1.9.14. ≠a United States ≠x History ≠y French and Indian War, 1755-1763.
≠y Casualties.

1.9.15. ≠a China ≠x History ≠y T'ang dynasty, 618-907.

1.9.16. ≠a Canada ≠x History ≠y Confederation, 1867.
≠a Confederation of Canada, 1867 ≠x History.

1.9.17. ≠a Greece ≠x History ≠y War of Independence, 1821-1829.

1.9.18. ≠a France ≠x History ≠y Revolution, 1789-1799 ≠x Censorship.

1.9.19. ≠a Germany ≠x History ≠y Revolution, 1918 ≠x Posters.

1.9.20. ≠a France ≠x History ≠y Reign of Terror, 1793-1794 ≠x Juvenile literature.

1.9.21. ≠a Canada ≠x History ≠y Rebellion, 1837-1838 ≠x Campaigns.

1.9.22. ≠a United States ≠x History ≠y Revolution, 1775-1783 ≠x Battlefields
≠x Juvenile literature.

1.9.23. ≠a China ≠x History ≠y Five Dynasties and the Ten Kingdoms, 907-979.

1.9.24. ≠a Germany ≠x History ≠y Unification, 1990 ≠x Bibliography.

1.9.25. ≠a Greece ≠x History ≠y 323-1453.

1.9.26. ≠a China ≠x History ≠y Ming dynasty, 1368-1644 ≠x Historiography.

1.9.27. ≠a Canada ≠x History ≠y 1945-
≠a Canadian Spy Trials, Canada, 1946.

1.9.28. ≠a France ≠x History ≠y February Revolution, 1848.

1.9.29.   ‡a Greece ‡x History ‡y Revolution, 1848 ‡x Bibliography.

1.9.30.   ‡a United States ‡x History ‡y 1801-1809 ‡x Fiction.
          ‡a Burr-Hamilton Duel, Weehawken, N.J., 1804 ‡x Fiction.

1.9.31.   ‡a Germany ‡x History, Military ‡y 19th century.

1.9.32.   ‡a China ‡x History ‡y Cultural Revolution, 1966-1969 ‡x Pictorial works.

1.9.33.   ‡a France ‡x History ‡y 1958- ‡x Bibliography.

1.9.34.   ‡a United States ‡x History, Naval ‡x Anecdotes.

1.9.35.   ‡a Greece ‡x History ‡y 1950-1967 ‡x Juvenile literature.

1.10. Biography Subdivisions Exercise Answers

1.10.1.   No. Often little is known of the personal details of their lives.

1.10.2.   Two—the name of the letter writer and the name of the addressee.

1.10.3.   None, unless the focus is on only one or two. In that case, bring out the one or two primary persons.

1.10.4.   Classes of persons, ethnic groups, names of individual corporate bodies, and names of individual persons, including literary authors.

1.10.5.   If appropriate, a "class of persons" heading; headings to bring out the person's association with a place or organization, or involvement with a specific event; topical headings.

1.10.6.   This type of heading benefits library users who are seeking biographies of a particular type of person rather than a particular individual. If the biographee belongs to no discernible class of persons likely to be sought by the typical public library user, it may be omitted.

1.10.7.   No more than two.

1.10.8.   Yes, when the work being cataloged is a general collection of interviews with persons from a wide variety of groups or undesignated backgrounds. Do not use it as both heading and subdivision at the same time.

1.10.9.   Assign more than one if a single heading cannot adequately encompass the person's career or pursuits. If a work focuses on only one facet, assign only that one heading.

1.10.10. Yes.

1.10.11. No. In those cases, the established subdivisions take precedence over the free-floating list.

1.10.12. Only if the sex or ethnic group is a significant aspect of the work. If assigned, it must be in addition to the unqualified heading for the class of persons.

1.10. Biography Subdivisions Exercise Answers

1.10.13. No.

1.10.14. No. Use the closest subdivision from the list in *SCM:SH*.

1.10.15. Yes, if the collective biography encompasses a group of people for which a heading representing a class of persons does not exist and cannot be formulated.

1.10.16. Only when the collection is by more than one writer and when the letters are classed as literary works.

1.10.17. No.

1.10.18. Use the subdivisions from the field in which the person is better known. If the person is better known as a literary author, use the subdivisions from H 1155.4.

1.10.19. Only when the place, organization, or event is a significant aspect of the work.

1.10.20. Registers or records of personal experiences, observations, thoughts, or feelings, kept daily or at frequent intervals.

1.10.21. Yes. They are designated with an asterisk.

1.10.22. No.

1.10.23. Three headings: Name of the diarist, class of persons or ethnic group, topical headings for any special topics discussed in the diary.

1.10.24. No.

1.10.25. Section H 1155.2.

1.10.26. Yes.

1.10.27. H 1720, part 3.

1.10.28. --**Diaries**.

1.10.29. Yes. As the list is intended to apply to all literary authors, certain subdivisions occur that would not apply to Shakespeare, but may apply to other literary authors.

1.10.30. Yes.

1.10.31. *SCM:SH* H 1581, section 3.c.

1.10.32. No. Prefer the "class of persons" heading.

1.10.33. Yes.

1.10.34. A partial biography.

1.10.35. Yes.

1.10.36. Two headings: **Barbara Bush; Presidents' spouses--United States--Biography.**

1.10.37. Four headings: **John Kennedy, Jr.; Caroline Kennedy; Jacqueline Kennedy; Presidents--United States--Family.**

1.10.38. Two headings: **Paul "Bear" Bryant; Football coaches--Biography.**

1.10.39. Two headings: **Henry VIII--Family; Kings and rulers--England--Family.**

1.10.40. One heading: **French letters.**

1.10.41. Four headings: **Cajuns--Louisiana--Correspondence; Cajuns--Korea--Correspondence; Korean War, 1950-1953--Personal narratives, American; Louisiana--Biography.**

1.10.42. Four headings: **Pickering, Sam--Correspondence; Pickering, Tom--Correspondence; Horse breeders--Virginia--Correspondence; Race horses--Breeding.**

1.10.43. Three headings: **Frontier and pioneer life--Oregon Trail--Diaries; Pioneers--Oregon Trail--Diaries; Oregon Trail--Biography.**

1.11. Bible Headings and Subdivisions Exercise Answers

1.11.1. Works about the Bible, works on special topics discussed in the Bible, and works on the theological and ethical teachings of the Bible.

1.11.2. *Versions* are translations of particular sacred books and their parts. These translations are generally made from original texts, although in some instances a modern translation is made from an earlier version.

1.11.3. A work that criticizes or comments on another work. It can be published independently or in conjunction with the text of the original work.

1.11.4. Yes.

1.11.5. Use **--Translating.**

1.11.6. Use **--Commentaries.**

1.11.7. Use **[topic] in the Bible** for this type of work.

1.11.8. Use **--Versions.**

1.11.9. Yes.

1.11.10. Yes, both are acceptable.

1.11.11. Use this subdivision for translations of a sacred book or its parts into languages belonging to that group (or another *group* of languages). Do not assign this heading for an individual language.

1.11.12. Use **Bible. Nepalese--Versions.**

1.11.13. Use **Bible. Nepalese--Versions, Lutheran.**

1.11.14. Only under **Bible. O.T.** or its individual books.

1.11.15. Use --Biblical teaching.

1.11.16. Only under **Bible. O.T.** or its individual books.

1.11.17. Only under **Bible. N.T.** or its individual books.

1.11.18. Two headings: **Salvation--Biblical teaching; Bible. N.T. Mark--Criticism, interpretation, etc.**

1.11.19. Two headings: **Parenting--Biblical teaching; Parenting--Religious aspects.**

1.11.20. Three headings: **Clothing and dress--Religious aspects; Biblical costume; Apostles--Costume.**

1.11.21. One heading: **Bible--Versions, Chinese--Bibliography.**

1.12. Special Subdivisions from *SCM:SH* Exercise Answers

1.12.1. Works consisting entirely of pictures or of pictures accompanied only by captions.

1.12.2. As something noteworthy that occurs or occurred in a certain place during a discrete interval of time.

1.12.3. No.

1.12.4. No.

1.12.5. At least 50% of the work.

1.12.6. No.

1.12.7. Twenty-five. **Accidents; Weddings.**

1.12.8. Nineteen. **Athletic contests; Tournaments.**

1.12.9. Thirteen. The first three given are **--Antiquities, --Biography,** and **--Church history.**

1.12.10. **--Genealogy** or **--History.**

1.12.11. **--Foreign public opinion.**

1.12.12. No.

1.12.13. **--Description and travel--Views; --Description--Views.**

1.12.14. Name, locality, and date.

1.12.15. No, only for unique events. If the event spanned a period of more than one year, specify the full range of years.

1.12.16. Works on the study of the origin, descent, and relationship of named families, especially those dealing with family papers, deeds, wills, public records, parish registers, cemetery inscriptions, ship lists, etc.

1.12.17. No.

1.12.18. **--Portraits.**

1.12.19. Yes, if the event focuses entirely on an individual corporate body.

1.12.20. Yes, if the work deals with materials from the entire country or continent.

1.12.21. Yes, the free-floating subdivisions in Section H 1140 may be used for works on the history of religion in a place during a particular time period.

1.12.22. *SCM:SH* section H 1659.

1.12.23. Those aspects of culture that are learned orally, by imitation, or by observation, including traditional beliefs, narratives (tales, legends, proverbs, etc.), folk medicine, and other aspects of the expressive performance and communication involved in oral tradition.

1.12.24. No, only for those below country level, such as a city, county, state, region, etc.

1.12.25. The individual religion is subdivided by the place.

1.12.26. No.

1.12.27. Yes, but not at the same time.

1.12.28. Six subjects: Activities, Archaeological evidence, Classes of persons, Monuments and memorials, Particular uses of land and historic structures, and Historic events.

1.12.29. Yes.

1.12.30. No. The name of the theologian is assigned without further subdivision.

1.12.31. A form subdivision—it tells you something about the format of the work.

1.12.32. No, the practice of assigning both headings has been discontinued.

1.12.33. Under non-religious or non-ethical topics to designate works that discuss the topic from the religious standpoint.

1.12.34. Both.

1.12.35. When the work you are cataloging consists of actual photographs (not photographic reproductions).

1.12.36. No, the practice has been discontinued.

1.12.37. The predominant attitude of a community of people on a topic.

1.12.38. No. **--Religion** would be used for these groups.

1.12.39. No, they are inherently folkloric, and to use the subdivision would be redundant.

1.12.40. Yes.

1.12.41. Under non-religious or non-ethical topics to designate works that discuss the topic as a theme in mythology.

1.12.42. The heading **Fairy tales** is usually assigned to narratives dealing with supernatural beings or supernatural events, and which are often created for the amusement of children. The heading **Legends** usually deals with narratives regarded by their tellers as true. They may be religious or supernatural in nature, and deal with individuals or specific places.

1.12.43. For traditional narratives that are for the most part fictitious and are told primarily for entertainment.

1.12.44. --Attitudes.

1.12.45. Under non-religious or non-ethical works that discuss the moral and/or ethical questions regarding the topic.

2.1. *Sears* Subject Heading Exercise Answers

These are suggested answers. You may have others that also fit the description given in the exercise.

2.1.1.   A.   Long, Huey Pierce, 1893-1935.
       B.   Louisiana--Politics and government.
       C.   Governors--Louisiana--Biography.

2.1.2.   A.   Louisiana. Dept. of Education--History.
       B.   Education--Louisiana--History.
       C.   Education and state.
       D.   Louisiana--Officials and employees.

2.1.3.   A.   Tunica Indians--Social life and customs.
       B.   Biloxi Indians--Social life and customs.
       C.   Indians of North America--Southern States--Social life and customs.

2.1.4.   A.   African-Americans--United States--History--1861-1865, Civil War.
       B.   United States. Army.
       C.   United States--History--1861-1865, Civil War.

2.1.5.   A.   New Orleans (La.)--Social life and customs.
       B.   Plantation life.
       C.   Historic buildings--Louisiana--New Orleans.

2.1.6.   A.   Offshore oil well drilling--Law and legislation.
       B.   Petroleum--Law and legislation.
       C.   Marine mineral resources--Law and legislation.
       D.   Petroleum industry--Law and legislation.
       E.   Offshore oil industry--Law and legislation.
       F.   Mexico, Gulf of--Law and legislation.

2.1.7.   A. Library architecture.
         B. Architecture--Awards.
         C. Libraries--Louisiana.

2.1.8.   A. Hebert family.
         B. New Orleans (La.)--Genealogy.
         C. New Orleans (La.)--Biography.

2.1.9.   A. Mines and mineral resources--Law and legislation.
         B. Hazardous waste sites--Law and legislation.
         C. Hazardous wastes--Law and legislation.

2.1.10. A. Roads--Environmental aspects.
         B. Highway transportation--Planning.
         C. Traffic engineering--Planning.
         D. Cobb County (Ga.)--Planning.

2.1.11. A. Flood control.
         B. Drainage.
         C. Floods--Pennsylvania--Johnstown.

2.1.12. A. School attendance--History.
         B. Florida Parishes (La.)--History.
         C. Education--Louisiana--Florida Parishes--History.

2.1.13. A. Arpadhon (La.)--History.
         B. Arpadhon (La.)--Biography.
         C. Hungarian Americans--Louisiana--Arpadhon.

2.1.14. A. Sarajevo (Bosnia and Hercegovina)--Politics and government.
         B. Sarajevo (Bosnia and Hercegovina)--History--Siege, 1992-
         C. Bosnians--Personal narratives.

2.1.15. A. Persian Gulf War, 1991.
         B. Military transportation.
         C. United States. Army--Military life.

2.1.16. A. Printing--Germany--History.
         B. Books--History.
         C. Typesetting--History.

2.1.17. A. AIDS (Disease)--Case studies.
         B. Hospices--Case studies.
         C. AIDS (Disease)--Treatment--Case studies.

2.1.18. A. Euthanasia.
         B. Medical ethics.
         C. Death--Religious aspects.

2.1. *Sears* Subject Heading Exercise Answers

2.1.19. A. Great Wall of China (China)--History.
B. China--History.
C. Fortification.

2.1.20. A. Nixon, Richard M. (Richard Milhous), 1913-
B. Presidents--United States--Biography.
C. Governors--California--Biography.

2.1.21. A. Richmond (Va.)--Social life and customs.
B. Plantation life.
C. Historic buildings--Virginia--Richmond.

2.1.22. A. Missoula (Mont.). Office of the Mayor--History.
B. Missoula (Mont.)--Politics and government.
C. Municipal government--Montana--Missoula.

2.1.23. A. Cherokee Indians--Social life and customs.
B. Marriage customs and rites.
C. Cherokee Indians--Women--Social life and customs.

2.1.24. A. Alabama--History--1861-1865, Civil War.
B. Veterans--Alabama.
C. Alabama--Genealogy.

2.1.25. A. Pipelines--Design and construction.
B. Pipelines--Alaska--Maintenance and repair.
C. Trans-Alaska Pipeline--History.

2.1.26. A. Louisiana irises--Encyclopedias.
B. Irises--Encyclopedias.
C. Ornamental plants--Encyclopedias.

2.1.27. A. Junk bonds--Law and legislation.
B. Bonds--Rating--Law and legislation.
C. Stock exchange--Law and legislation.

2.1.28. A. Whitefield family.
B. Shawnee (Kans.)--Biography.
C. Shawnee (Kans.)--Genealogy.

2.1.29. A. Hurricane Andrew, 1992.
B. Hurricanes--Florida.
C. Hurricanes--Louisiana.

2.1.30. A. Canals--New York--History--19th century.
B. Erie Canal (N.Y.)--History--19th century.
C. Inland navigation--History--19th century.
D. Freight--History--19th century.

2.1.31. A. Isleto Indians--New Mexico--History.
        B. New Mexico--Ethnic relations.
        C. Frontier and pioneer life--New Mexico.

2.1.32. A. Bridges--Missouri--Saint Louis--Planning.
        B. Highway engineering--Missouri--Saint Louis--Citizen participation.
        C. Bridges--Mississippi River--Planning.

2.1.33. A. All terrain vehicles--Maintenance and repair.
        B. Dune buggies--Maintenance and repair.
        C. Snowmobiles--Maintenance and repair.

2.1.34. A. Mount Everest Expedition, 1922.
        B. Mount Everest Expedition, 1924.
        C. Mount Everest Expedition, 1938.
        D. Everest, Mount (China and Nepal)--Description.
        E. Mountaineering.

2.1.35. A. Panizzi, Anthony.
        B. Librarians--Biography.
        C. British Museum--History.

2.1.36. A. Architectural decoration and ornament--Design and construction.
        B. Architecture--Details.
        C. Architecture--Designs and plans.

2.2. *Sears* Subject Heading Terminology and Scope Notes Exercise Answers

2.2.1. America--Antiquities
        Antiques
        Bible--Antiquities
        Chicago (Ill.)--Antiquities
        Christian antiquities
        Classical antiquities
        Egypt--Antiquities
        Indians of North America--Antiquities
        Jews--Antiquities
        Ohio--Antiquities
        Prehistoric peoples
        United States--Antiquities

2.2.2. Civil engineering
        Engineering

2.2.3. Cinema
        Films

2.2. Sears Subject Heading Terminology and Scope Notes

         Movies
         Moving pictures
         Talking pictures

2.2.4. Names of countries with the subhead "Navy" or the subdivision "Naval history", e.g., **United States. Navy; United States--Naval history**; etc. to be added as necessary.
         Naval art and science
         Naval battles
         United States. Navy
         Warships
         Naval history
         Navies

2.2.5. Algebras, Linear

2.2.6. Bicycles
         Cycling

2.2.7. Yes.

2.2.8. No.

2.2.9. No.

2.2.10. Use for materials on the scientific study of speech and for comparative studies of languages. General materials on the history, philosophy, origin, etc., of languages are entered under **Language and languages**.

2.2.11. Types of berries, e.g., **Strawberries**; to be added as needed, in the plural form.

2.2.12. No.

2.2.13. Yes, **History of different periods**.

2.2.14. Yes.

2.2.15. No.

2.2.16. Yes.

2.2.17. Insurgency, Military art and science, Tactics, War.

2.2.18. Home Box Office.

2.2.19. Guide dogs--Training.

2.2.20. Yes.

2.2.21. **French language--Composition and exercises**.

2.2.22. Yes.

2.2.23. By reading the scope note under **Rhetoric**.

2.2.24. Those above the secondary level.

2.2.25. Yes.

2.2.26. Signs and symbols.

2.2.27. Flags, Heraldry, Insignia, Mottoes, Seals (Numismatics), State emblems.

2.2.28. Yes.

2.2.29. No.

2.2.30. Hazardous occupations.

2.2.31. **Constitutional history** and **Constitutions**.

2.2.32. The scope notes under SA (*See Also*) references will tell you that headings can be added as needed.

2.2.33. End of the world.

2.2.34. Inorganic chemistry.

2.2.35. **Direct selling** and **Marketing**.

2.2.36. Yes.

2.2.37. No.

2.2.38. Minerals.

2.2.39. Geology.

2.3. *Sears* History Subdivisions Exercise Answers

2.3.1. ≠a Germany ≠x History ≠y 0-1517.

2.3.2. ≠a China ≠x History ≠x Humor.

2.3.3. ≠a United States ≠x History ≠y 1600-1775, Colonial period.

2.3.4. ≠a Canada ≠x History ≠y 1763-1867.

2.3.5. ≠a France ≠x History ≠y 0-1328.

2.3.6. ≠a Greece ≠x History ≠y 0-323.

2.3.7. ≠a Germany ≠x History ≠y 0-1517.

2.3.8. ≠a France ≠x History ≠y 0-1328.

2.3.9. ≠ a China ≠x History.

2.3.10. ≠a Canada ≠x History ≠y 1800-1899 (19th century) ≠x Juvenile literature.

2.3.11. ≠a Greece ≠x History ≠y 0-323.

3.1. Dewey Relative Index Exercise Answers

2.3.12. ≠a United States ≠x History ≠y 1689-1697, King William's War.

2.3.13. ≠a Germany ≠x History ≠y 1815-1866.

2.3.14. ≠a United States ≠x History ≠y 1755-1763, French and Indian War.

2.3.15. ≠a China ≠x History.

2.3.16. ≠a Canada ≠x History ≠y 1763-1867.

2.3.17. ≠a Greece ≠x History ≠y 1453-

2.3.18. ≠a France ≠x History ≠y 1789-1799, Revolution ≠x Censorship.

2.3.19. ≠a Germany ≠x History ≠y 1866-1918.

2.3.20. ≠a France ≠x History ≠y 1789-1799, Revolution ≠x Juvenile literature.

2.3.21. ≠a Canada ≠x History ≠y 1763-1867.

2.3.22. ≠a United States ≠x History ≠y 1775-1783, Revolution ≠x Juvenile literature.

2.3.23. ≠a China ≠x History.

2.3.24. ≠a Germany ≠x History ≠y 1990- ≠x Bibliography.

2.3.25. ≠a Greece ≠x History ≠y 323-1453.

2.3.26. ≠a China ≠x History ≠x Historiography.

2.3.27. ≠a Canada ≠x History ≠y 1945-

2.3.28. ≠a France ≠x History ≠y 1815-1914.

2.3.29. ≠a Greece ≠x History ≠y 1453- ≠x Bibliography.

2.3.30. ≠a United States ≠x History ≠y 1783-1865.

2.3.31. ≠a China ≠x History ≠y 1949- ≠x Pictorial works.

2.3.32. ≠a France ≠x History ≠y 1958-1969 ≠x Bibliography.

2.3.33. ≠a United States ≠x Naval history ≠x Anecdotes.

2.3.34. ≠a Greece ≠x History ≠y 1453- ≠x Juvenile literature.

3.1. Dewey Relative Index Exercise Answers

3.1.1. Dewey: 363.7063

3.1.2. Dewey: 016.9763

3.1.3. Dewey: 615.1

3.1.4. Dewey: 574.52642

3.1.5. Dewey: 798.25079

Answer Key

3.1.6.   Dewey: 746.46
3.1.7.   Dewey: 636.085
3.1.8.   Dewey: 621.69
3.1.9.   Dewey: 386.48
3.1.10. Dewey: 621.59
3.1.11. Dewey: 333.9162
3.1.12. Dewey: 949.501
3.1.13. Dewey: 734.224
3.1.14. Dewey: 635.92
3.1.15. Dewey: 745.5924
3.1.16. Dewey: 363.12514

3.2. Dewey Schedules Exercise Answers

3.2.1.   641.5
3.2.2.   641.512
3.2.3.   641.568
3.2.4.   641.572
3.2.5.   641.59763
3.2.6.   641.813
3.2.7.   641.852
3.2.8.   641.875
3.2.9.   641.8653
3.2.10. 641.5638
3.2.11. 291
3.2.12. 230
3.2.13. 232.9
3.2.14. 291.24
3.2.15. 226.4
3.2.16. 269.2
3.2.17. 252.53
3.2.18. 246.1

3.2. Dewey Schedules Exercise Answers

3.2.19.	235.2
3.2.20.	296.09
3.2.21.	790.068
3.2.22.	791.3
3.2.23.	791.4303
3.2.24.	791.4367
3.2.25.	791.4375
3.2.26.	794.1
3.2.27.	796.332
3.2.28.	797.122
3.2.29.	799.14
3.2.30.	799.26
3.2.31.	629.222
3.2.32.	629.2872
3.2.33.	629.22042
3.2.34.	796.72
3.2.35.	778.949629222
3.2.36.	796.79
3.2.37.	363.125
3.2.38.	346.038
3.2.39.	343.0944
3.2.40.	636.1
3.2.41.	682.1
3.2.42.	798.4
3.2.43.	595.773
3.2.44.	357.1
3.2.45.	388.46
3.2.46.	688.78
3.2.47.	796.353
3.2.48.	779.943296655
3.2.49.	363.75

124 Answer Key

3.2.50.   387.2

3.2.51.   623.8223

3.2.52.   623.87234

3.2.53.   743.9493872

3.2.54.   797.1246

3.2.55.   343.0968

3.2.56.   363.123

3.2.57.   363.286

3.2.58.   623.8938

3.2.59.   386.2234

3.2.60.   623.865

3.3. Number Building Exercise Answers

3.3.1.   Base number   778.9
         Full number from which a part will be taken   704.9432
         Numbers to be added   32
         Final call number   778.932

3.3.2.   Base number   387.2
         Full number from which a part will be taken   623.8224
         Numbers to be added   24
         Final call number   387.224

3.3.3.   Base number   794.8
         Full number from which a part will be taken   796.332
         Numbers to be added   6332
         Final call number   794.86332

3.3.4.   Base number   266
         Full number from which a part will be taken   282
         Numbers to be added   2
         Final call number   266.2

3.3. Number Building Exercise Answers

3.3.5.
Base number	387.73
Full number from which a part will be taken	629.133347
Numbers to be added	347
Final call number	387.73347

3.3.6.
Base number	632.6
Full number from which a part will be taken	595.7648
Numbers to be added	57648
Final call number	632.657648

3.3.7.
Base number	523.98
Full number from which a part will be taken	523.46
Numbers to be added	6
Final call number	523.986

3.3.8.
Base number	355.82
Full number from which a part will be taken	623.445
Numbers to be added	45
Final call number	355.8245

3.3.9.
Base number	629.221
Full number from which a part will be taken	629.2252
Numbers to be added	52
Final call number	629.22152

3.3.10.
Base number	743.6
Full number from which a part will be taken	598.442
Numbers to be added	8442
Final call number	743.68442

3.3.11.
Base number	242.80
Full number from which a part will be taken	285
Numbers to be added	5
Final call number	242.805

3.3.12.
Base number	612.6401
Full number from which a part will be taken	611.12
Numbers to be added	12
Final call number	612.640112

126   Answer Key

3.3.13. Base number — 153.94
Full number from which a part will be taken — 786.2
Numbers to be added — 7862
Final call number — 153.947862

3.3.14. Base number — 622.18
Full number from which a part will be taken — 553.4629
Numbers to be added — 4629
Final call number — 622.184629

3.3.15. Base number — 333.85
Full number from which a part will be taken — 553.668
Numbers to be added — 668
Final call number — 333.85668

3.3.16. Base number — 639.37
Full number from which a part will be taken — 597.73
Numbers to be added — 73
Final call number — 639.3773

3.3.17. Base number — 371.07
Full number from which a part will be taken — 299.561
Numbers to be added — 9561
Final call number — 371.079561

3.3.18. Base number — 551.64
Full number from which a part will be taken — 551.559
Numbers to be added — 59
Final call number — 551.6459

3.3.19. Base number — 688.79
Full number from which a part will be taken — 799.202834
Numbers to be added — 202834
Final call number — 688.79202834

3.3.20. Base number — 016
Full number from which a part will be taken — 621.3815483
Numbers to be added — 6213815483
Final call number — 016.6213815483

3.4. Number Building from Tables Exercise Answers

Table 1

3.4.1. Base number — 666.3
Notation from Table 1 — -03
Numbers to be added — 3
Final call number — 666.33

3.4.2. Base number — 666.13
Notation from Table 1 — -0286
Numbers to be added — 6
Final call number — 666.136

3.4.3. Base number — 359
Notation from Table 1 — -0683
Numbers to be added — 00683
Final call number — 359.00683

3.4.4. Base number — 792.029
Notation from Table 1 — -0687
Numbers to be added — 687
Final call number — 792.029687

Table 2

3.4.5. Base number — 383.49
Notation from Table 2 — -515
Numbers to be added — 515
Final call number — 383.49515

3.4.6. Base number — 020.624
Notation from Table 2 — -763452
Numbers to be added — 763452
Final call number — 020.624763452

3.4.7. Base number — 133.129
Notation from Table 2 — -747277
Numbers to be added — 747277
Final call number — 133.129747277

128 Answer Key

3.4.8. Base number — 263.042
Notation from Table 2 — -42234
Numbers to be added — 42234
Final call number — 263.04242234

Table 3-A

3.4.9. Base number — 84
Notation from Table 3-A — -2
Numbers to be added — 2
Final call number — 842

3.4.10. Base number — 86
Notation from Table 3-A — -1
Numbers to be added — 1
Final call number — 861

3.4.11. Base number — 83
Notation from Table 3-A — -3
Numbers to be added — 3
Final call number — 833

Table 3-B

3.4.12. Base number — 808.1
Notation from Table 3-B — -1032
Numbers to be added — 32
Final call number — 808.132

3.4.13. Base number — 808.83
Notation from Table 3-B — -3087
Numbers to be added — 87
Final call number — 808.8387

3.4.14. Base number — 808.82
Notation from Table 3-B — -20527
Numbers to be added — 527
Final call number — 808.82527

3.4. Number Building from Tables Exercise Answers

Table 3-C

3.4.15.
Base number	808.80
Notation from Table 3-C	-375
Numbers to be added	375
Final call number	808.80375

3.4.16.
Base number	808.879
Notation from Table 3-C	-352
Numbers to be added	352
Final call number	808.879352

3.4.17.
Base number	808.859
Notation from Table 3-C	-355
Numbers to be added	355
Final call number	808.859355

Table 4

3.4.18.
Base number	430.04
Notation from Table 4	-5
Numbers to be added	5
Final call number	430.045

3.4.19.
Base number	440.04
Notation from Table 4	-864
Numbers to be added	864
Final call number	440.04864

3.4.20.
Base number	491.43
Notation from Table 4	-31
Numbers to be added	31
Final call number	491.4331

Table 5

3.4.21.
Base number	704.03
Notation from Table 5	-9992
Numbers to be added	9992
Final call number	704.039992

3.4.22.	Base number	155.457
	Notation from Table 5	-942
	Numbers to be added	942
	Final call number	155.457942
3.4.23.	Base number	133.593
	Notation from Table 5	-9712
	Numbers to be added	9712
	Final call number	133.5939712

Table 6

3.4.24.	Base number	033
	Notation from Table 6	-3961
	Numbers to be added	961
	Final call number	033.961
3.4.25.	Base number	479
	Notation from Table 6	-797
	Numbers to be added	7
	Final call number	479.7
3.4.26.	Base number	398.204
	Notation from Table 6	-491
	Numbers to be added	491
	Final call number	398.204491

Table 7

3.4.27.	Base number	704
	Notation from Table 7	-08161
	Numbers to be added	08161
	Final call number	704.08161
3.4.28.	Base number	305.43
	Notation from Table 7	-3633
	Numbers to be added	3633
	Final call number	305.433633
3.4.29.	Base number	390.4
	Notation from Table 7	-551
	Numbers to be added	551
	Final call number	390.4551

3.5. Cutter Table Exercise Answers

3.5.1.   J724
3.5.2.   F381
3.5.3.   C672
3.5.4.   W725
3.5.5.   W332
3.5.6.   L585
3.5.7.   M332
3.5.8.   SH237
3.5.9.   SH232
3.5.10. SP22
3.5.11. V439
3.5.12. D38
3.5.13. B692
3.5.14. R541
3.5.15. SE56
3.5.16. P277
3.5.17. B855
3.5.18. SE89
3.5.19. EA77
3.5.20. M364
3.5.21. IN8
3.5.22. UP2
3.5.23. OC5
3.5.24. AL53
3.5.25. Y85
3.5.26. SM66
3.5.27. Z38
3.5.28. K837
3.5.29. EW55
3.5.30. L461
3.5.31. M465
3.5.32. F496

4.1. LCC Author Cutter Exercise Answers

4.1.1.	S77
4.1.2.	G67
4.1.3.	M55
4.1.4.	M35
4.1.5.	L36
4.1.6.	H67
4.1.7.	L38
4.1.8.	D47
4.1.9.	M67
4.1.10.	V36
4.1.11.	W55
4.1.12.	S53
4.1.13.	F87
4.1.14.	S65
4.1.15.	F69
4.1.16.	D49
4.1.17.	A94
4.1.18.	L44
4.1.19.	R67
4.1.20.	S74
4.1.21.	F74
4.1.22.	H35
4.1.23.	C85
4.1.24.	S74
4.1.25.	A53
4.1.26.	D54
4.1.27.	P38
4.1.28.	H39
4.1.29.	L36
4.1.30.	R44
4.1.31.	M33
4.1.32.	W38
4.1.33.	B68
4.1.34.	S69
4.1.35.	B76

4.2. LCC Outline Exercise Answers

4.2.1.	PN-PZ	
4.2.2.	PJ-PM	
4.2.3.	U	
4.2.4.	Z	
4.2.5.	R	
4.2.6.	PT	
4.2.7.	KF	
4.2.8.	BL-BX	
4.2.9.	J	
4.2.10.	N	
4.2.11.	V	
4.2.12.	L	
4.2.13.	H	
4.2.14.	E-F	
4.2.15.	S	

4.3. LCC Exercises, Set 1 Answers

4.3.1.	HV8555.S26 1997
4.3.2.	TX809.M17R58 1995
4.3.3.	TX736.S78 1997
4.3.4.	JC481.L46 1996
4.3.5.	UA845.E33 1994
4.3.6.	E884.L49 1991
4.3.7.	KF9223.K68 1996
4.3.8.	HV6252.T47 1997
4.3.9.	QP86.A97 1996
4.3.10.	DT61.B47 1997
4.3.11.	PN1998.3.H38M33 1997
4.3.12.	HE9803.Z7H57 1996
4.3.13.	HF5549.5.D55W37 1997
4.3.14.	PN4874.M377S65 1996
4.3.15.	GV964.W66S77 1997

4.3.16.	PN2778.B47S66 1996
4.3.17.	VG94.F6M36 1994
4.3.18.	KF8745.W3A3 1989
4.3.19.	HV6604.C72J56 1996
4.3.20.	D15.T65 1997

4.4. LCC Exercises, Set 2 Answers

4.4.1.	RC523.2
4.4.2.	RC552.E18
4.4.3.	NC1429.L37A4
4.4.4.	TT390
4.4.5.	TT323
4.4.6.	HQ1063.2.U6
4.4.7.	RJ135
4.4.8.	HD7125
4.4.9.	PN4305.M8
4.4.10.	PA4417
4.4.11.	LB1047.3
4.4.12.	HV1569.3W65
4.4.13.	BF385
4.4.14.	BF1093
4.4.15.	BL782
4.4.16.	GT3040
4.4.17.	CS2377
4.4.18.	PN1661
4.4.19.	RC931.O67
4.4.20.	TX773
4.4.21.	HQ21
4.4.22.	PN1993.5.U6
4.4.23.	GN281
4.4.24.	HV1780.4
4.4.25.	JV6465
4.4.26.	E221
4.4.27.	HV6524
4.4.28.	QE862.D5

4.4. LCC Exercises, Set 2 Answers

4.4.29.	HQ1064.U5
4.4.30.	RC607.A26
4.4.31.	HD9397.U52
4.4.32.	BX1406.2
4.4.33.	DG975.P25
4.4.34.	DS259.2
4.4.35.	E841
4.4.36.	R726
4.4.37.	RA601.5
4.4.38.	PN2287.D49
4.4.39.	HV9106.C4
4.4.40.	ML3524
4.4.41.	PN2287.R67
4.4.42.	RC268.25
4.4.43.	HV6773.2
4.4.44.	RM275
4.4.45.	ML420.S67
4.4.46.	CS2695
4.4.47.	CJ1836
4.4.48.	PN1998.A1
4.4.49.	LB2351.52
4.4.50.	KF311.Z9
4.4.51.	HM51
4.4.52.	HF5383
4.4.53.	HQ799.15
4.4.54.	QB602
4.4.55.	T21
4.4.56.	TT197
4.4.57.	TX837
4.4.58.	TT197.5.T3
4.4.59.	RM237.7